D0827897

Our Great
GOD AND
SAVIOUR

Our Great GOD AND SAVIOUR

Eric J. Alexander

THE BANNER OF TRUTH TRUST

THE BANNER OF TRUTH TRUST
3 Murrayfield Road, Edinburgh EH12 6EL, UK
P.O. Box 621, Carlisle, PA 17013, USA

*

© Eric J. Alexander 2010

*

ISBN-13: 978 1 84871 084 9

*

Typeset in 11/15 Adobe Caslon Pro at
the Banner of Truth Trust, Edinburgh

Printed in the U.S.A. by
Versa Press, Inc.,
East Peoria, IL

Except where stated, Scripture quotations are from
THE HOLY BIBLE: NEW INTERNATIONAL VERSION,
© International Bible Society, 1973, 1978, 1984.

FOR
GRETA

CONTENTS

PART THREE

THE CHURCH OF GOD

FOREWORD

*I*T IS A VERY SPECIAL PRIVILEGE to introduce Eric Alexander's *Our Great God and Saviour*. Many who have been enriched by his ministry over the years will greet its publication with enthusiasm and read it with great pleasure.

Others, perhaps, less familiar with his long and distinguished preaching ministry, on reading these wonderfully rich, clear, and spiritually nourishing pages, will wonder why more of his biblical exposition is not already in print.

The answer to that question is, in part, that he has never viewed writing as his gift. But a fuller explanation requires a brief summary of Eric Alexander's life.

Brought up in Glasgow, Scotland, and coming to living faith in Christ in his teenage years — largely through the influence of his elder brother — he was originally planning a career in medicine, only to be divinely diverted during the first days of his studies in the University of Glasgow. Called to the ministry he turned his attention to completing his Master of Arts and then proceeded to the study of Divinity, which he completed with a level of distinction that paved the way for the pursuit of a doctorate. But once more the Lord's ways proved different. Eric's brother became mortally ill (I once heard him described as 'too good for this world'), and in that context Eric's own course turned to more immediate entry into pastoral ministry. He served for several years as an assistant minister in Glasgow; thereafter for some fifteen years he served as minister of Loudoun East Church in Newmilns,

Ayrshire, before serving for two decades as minister of St George's-Tron in the city centre of Glasgow.

In the broader context of his ministry, it could be said of Eric Alexander what was observed about one his own pastoral heroes, Robert Murray M'Cheyne: 'he was always preaching, always visiting, always praying.' Anyone who has had the privilege of observing him at close quarters (as I often have), in his commitment to making the Word of God plain, in whole-souled intercession for his people, in pastoral counselling and personal visitation, could not miss the fact that the work of feeding and caring for the flock was not only the primary burden, but the driving passion of his ministry. With the loving and prayerful support of his wife Greta and their children Ronald and Jennifer, Eric Alexander's ministry illustrated the apostolic commitment, 'we will give ourselves to prayer and the ministry of the word' (*Acts* 6:4). That vision was etched deeply into his own life and illustrated for the people he served, as countless individuals in his congregations, in the student and business world, throughout the United Kingdom and North America, and in the far-flung mission stations of the world, could bear testimony.

It is because these have been the salient features and the driving burden of his life that Eric Alexander was not — could not have been — always writing.

Paradoxically, of course, that is what invests these written pages with their value — they come from a lifetime of faithful, consistent, biblical exposition expressed in a rare and remarkable gospel-empowered eloquence.

In these pages, then, are encapsulated some of the grand motifs of Eric Alexander's ministry. If it is true (as it surely is) that 'Man's chief end is to glorify God and enjoy him for ever', this has stood at the epicentre of his biblical exposition. The Majesty of God, the glory of the Lord Jesus Christ, the riches of the ministry of the Holy Spirit, the need for new birth, faith and repentance, the privileges and the struggles of ongoing sanctification, the glory of heaven, the centrality of the Word of God and the intercession of his people, have been the great emphases in his preaching. Whether in his regular systematic exposition of books of the Bible to his congregations, in short series or individual messages at conferences throughout the world as diverse as the Keswick Convention in England, the Urbana Conferences, or the Philadelphia Conferences in the USA, or conferences for missionaries or students, what Paul calls 'the open manifestation of the truth' from Scripture has been the dominant motif of his preaching. And this has been marked by an Isaianic eloquence, grace, and sense of worship that has been one of God's gifts to his people through his ministry.

Those who owe a debt of gratitude to Eric Alexander are legion, and it may be unfitting for me to claim (to use Paul's words in a very different context!) 'I more'. Our first meeting took place in 1967, at an InterVarsity student gathering at which he was speaking. I had heard much about him from fellow students (who, as students sometimes do, breathed his name in the reverent tones reserved only for the greatly admired!).

What first struck me, however, when I somewhat shyly began to introduce myself to him, was that Eric Alexander had already found out my name. It is hard now to express in words how remarkable it seemed to me at the time that someone so well known to my friends would take the trouble to find out the name of an insignificant student. Two years later I shared with some twenty other students in a mission in his congregation in Newmilns and with each of them felt the indelible impression of his ministry and found my debt to him increasing exponentially. In later life, with my family, I sat under his ministry of the Word in St George's-Tron, Sunday after Sunday, Wednesday after Wednesday, in season and out of season, benefiting beyond calculation from the ministry of a good workman, a master chef of the food of God. So I could go on — were it not that others would want to claim primacy of place in indebtedness and give similar testimony to the debt they owe.

This is why it is a very special privilege to introduce these pages, and a great personal joy to think that many who have not heard Eric Alexander preach in person may here experience the next to second-best thing. 'Next to second-best thing'? Yes, for the next best thing might be to go to the website which his son, Ronald, has created: www.ericalexander.co.uk — where many of his expositions may be heard.

But for the moment, go to your favourite chair if you are not already sitting in it, turn the page, pray for God's blessing on what you are about to read, and prepare to enjoy a feast of good things.

SINCLAIR B. FERGUSON
The First Presbyterian Church
Columbia, South Carolina,
USA
May 2010

INTRODUCTION

T HE CONTENTS OF *Our Great God and Saviour*[1] are largely based on a series of studies prepared over the years in connection with the Philadelphia Conference on Reformed Theology (affectionately known as 'The PCRT'). Inaugurated and led for many years by my friend, the late Dr James Montgomery Boice, it continues to be held annually at Tenth Presbyterian Church, Philadelphia, and at various other venues throughout the United States under the auspices of the Alliance of Confessing Evangelicals. I am indebted to the Alliance, not only for the privilege of being a member of their Council, but for their ready willingness to have this material included in this book. Their web site is www.alliancenet.org, and their purpose is to call the twenty-first-century church to a new reformation.

The threefold division of the book is really a reflection of the fact that each PCRT week-end focuses on a particular theme of the theology of the Reformation. For example, in two successive years we concentrated on the Attributes of God: hence, Part 1 of this volume is devoted to that theme. In another year, the subject considered was the Salvation of God, which in this volume is the general theme of Part 2. In yet another year, our attention was turned to 'The Church as God's New Society'. That is the theme of Part 3 of this book.

The PCRT is a conference designed, not for academic theologians, but for thoughtful church members who are hungry for the

[1] Our title is taken from Titus 2:13.

truth of holy Scripture which was rediscovered at the Reformation, and which our Lord told his disciples was the instrument of
our sanctification (*John* 17:17).

A central feature of this book is that each chapter is really an
exposition of a passage or verse of Scripture. That implies that
readers should have an open Bible before them as well as an open
book. The real value of this book will be the measure in which it
helps you to understand and obey the truth of the Bible.

Of course, much of the material in this volume derives from
expositions first given in St George's-Tron Church, Glasgow,
where I had the privilege of being minister for twenty years until
1997. To that patient, stimulating and encouraging congregation I
owe an immeasurable debt.

Finally, I want to say a special 'Thank you' for the invaluable
help of several people in producing this book. I am most grateful
to my friend Iain Murray, whose idea the book was in the first
place. The staff of the Banner of Truth Trust have been immensely
helpful and constantly patient in all our contacts. I want also to
express my great gratitude to Sinclair Ferguson for his too gener-
ous foreword. I have cherished his friendship now for over forty
years, and thank God for his ministry.

Eric J. Alexander
Glasgow,
February 2010

PART ONE
THE CHARACTER OF GOD

I

THE GREATNESS OF GOD

*T*HERE IS NO GREATER THEME we could ever consider than 'The nature of the God of the Bible'. God himself has instructed us to prize such study above everything else in life:

> 'Let not the wise man boast of his wisdom or the strong man boast of his strength or the rich man boast of his riches, but let him who boasts boast about this: that he understands and knows me, that I am the LORD, who exercises kindness, justice and righteousness on earth, for in these I delight', declares the LORD (*Jer.* 9:23–24).

That is our concern in this study – not only to ponder together the glories of the character of God, but more than that, to come to know him in a deeper way.

One of the greatest works on the existence and attributes of God was written by the great Puritan Stephen Charnock some three hundred years ago. It was published posthumously by his literary trustees. When they were commending this work to the Christian public these men wrote:

> A mere contemplation of the divine excellences may afford much pleasure to any man who loves to exercise his reason. But if that be so, what incomparable sweetness ought believers to find in viewing and considering now these perfections which they will more fully behold hereafter, seeing what

manner of God – in whom they have a covenant interest – how wise and powerful, how great, good and holy he is. Indeed, if rich men delight to sum up their vast revenues, to read over their rentals, to look upon their hoards, how much more should the people of God please themselves in seeing how rich they are in having an immensely full and all-sufficient God as their inheritance.[1]

That is what we are to do together: behold the enormous wealth that is ours in the glory of the God who has come to us in Jesus Christ.

MAGNIFYING THE LORD TOGETHER

First we must consider the greatness of God. Or if you prefer to think of it in another way in which Scripture introduces us to it, we are concerned here 'to magnify the Lord together'. The Psalmist invites his fellows: 'O magnify the LORD with me, and let us exalt his name together' (*Psa.* 34:3, KJV).

What happens when we magnify something? We do not actually increase its size. When we magnify something we make its true nature clearer and more obvious to ourselves. That is what the psalmist means when he speaks of magnifying the name of God. He is saying that we are to make God more apparent to ourselves and others, and thus to develop a fuller awareness of the greatness and glory of his nature.

Psalm 145 issues a warning to all who would engage in this exercise: 'Great is the LORD and most worthy of praise; his greatness no one can fathom' (verse 3). We will find, therefore that, even when we have contemplated the nature and character of God, we have only come to the edges of his ways. We are always going to be like little

[1] Stephen Charnock, *The Attributes of God* (Grand Rapids: Baker Book House, reprint 1979), p. 19.

kindergarten children in the honours class of a university. Indeed, even when we see him face to face in glory, we will still never fully comprehend all the glory and greatness of God's character.

There are two corollaries of this truth that we need constantly to have in mind.

First, *we are absolutely dependent for all our knowledge of God on revelation*. Unless God reveals himself to us, we can know nothing of him. But God does reveal himself. That is a glorious reality. God has made himself known in creation, in his Son and in Holy Scripture. Scripture tells us what to think about creation and how to understand the life and work of Jesus. So for our understanding of God, we are absolutely dependent upon, and need to be submitted to, Scripture.

Second, *we are equally dependent upon the illumination of the Holy Spirit*. He must illumine the written revelation in our understanding so that with confidence, not in the wisdom of men but in God himself, we may discover something of his glory.

'THE LORD HAS SPOKEN'

We turn therefore, in this first chapter, to Isaiah 40. The fortieth chapter of Isaiah is a watershed of the prophecy. Isaiah is looking beyond his own time, some 150 to 200 years further on, to the desolate days when Israel was to be scattered, its temple destroyed, and the very cream of the nation taken captive.

What God reveals to Isaiah is that when the people are in this moribund condition, and the cause of God appears to be languishing, what is most needed is a fresh revelation of who God is in his true character. A new vision of God is, therefore, what Isaiah concentrates on.

God tells Isaiah to encourage Jerusalem and give her hope. The focus of that hope lies in the revelation of God's character. Thus a voice is heard calling out in the desert, 'Prepare the way for the LORD; make straight in the wilderness a highway for our God' (*Isa.* 40:3). The apex of the promise that the Lord himself is coming is reached in verse 5: 'The glory of the LORD will be revealed, and all mankind together will see it.'

That promise was fulfilled in the deliverance of God's people from the captivity of the Babylonian Exile. But the fulfilment was not exhausted then. It was ultimately fulfilled in a greater sense in the coming of our Lord Jesus Christ, whose forerunner, John the Baptist, quoted these very words, saying, 'I am the voice crying in the wilderness' (*John* 1:23).

Yet there is an even greater fulfilment of these words that still awaits us. For the glory of the Lord, which all mankind will see together, will come at that final revelation of glory when the Lord Jesus Christ returns at the end of the age. Then the ultimate glory of God will be manifested and every eye shall see it – in the face of Jesus.

But here the prophet says: 'Here is your God! See, the Sovereign Lord comes with power, and his arm rules for him' (*Isa.* 40:9–10).

The rest of this chapter is composed of prophetic insight into the incomparable greatness of this most sovereign Lord. The people to whom Isaiah is writing are a people who at the time envisaged would be in bondage; they would be in despair. They would have known the distress caused by being oppressed by their enemies. But God brings them this vision of himself as the cure for these burdens. As Professor John N. Oswalt puts it in his commentary on Isaiah: 'The prophet seems to be saying that if humanity could ever glimpse the true picture of God's greatness and glory, their problems would be on their way to being solved.'[1]

I believe that is true of our generation. There is nothing that the church of Jesus Christ needs more in our day than this fresh

[1] John N. Oswalt, *The Book of Isaiah, Chapters 1–39* (Grand Rapids: Eerdmans Publishing Company, 1986), p. 32.

revelation – an eye-opener – of the glory, majesty and wonder of God.

Isaiah displays the greatness of God in this passage by relating four elements:

1. God's uniqueness within the creation (verse 12)
2. God's independence from the creation (verses 13–14)
3. God's supremacy above the creation (verses 15–20), and
4. God's sovereignty over the creation (verses 21–24).

UNIQUENESS WITHIN THE CREATION

In verses 12–14 the prophet asks five unanswerable questions to establish the absolute uniqueness of God within, and the independence of God from, the created order. The first two deal with his uniqueness.

Who has measured the waters in the hollow of his hand, or with the breadth of his hand marked off the heavens? Who has held the dust of the earth in a basket, or weighed the mountains on the scales and the hills in a balance? (verse 12).

These questions relate to the measuring of creation, and they display God as both infinitely transcendent above his creation and unique within it. They are challenges to man in his littleness – to stop viewing God as though he were a person like ourselves.

That is one of the tendencies that often develops as we think about God in his personal nature. You may remember how the psalmist records God's complaint about this in Psalm 50:21. The people had lost their vision of God's greatness, and God says, 'You thought I was altogether like you.' This is why Isaiah asks, 'Who else holds the oceans in his hand to measure them?' This is what God does! 'Who else measures the heavens as a handbreadth or the soil of the earth in his basket, or holds the mountains in his scales to weigh them?'

Can you picture what Isaiah is saying of God? Can you think of God taking the mountains – Everest and the Eiger, for example – putting them in a balance and holding them to see which is heavier? Or again, can you think of the Lord God putting his hand on the heavens and measuring it with just a span? Isaiah asks, 'Who else has done this?'

Isaiah is trying to teach us about God's immensity. Is this not precisely what we have lost in so much of our thinking? It is one reason we need a new emphasis on the doctrine of God as Creator. This is how the men and women of the Bible enlarged their faith and fed it. They came into the presence of God, and then, like Jeremiah, they prayed: 'Ah, Sovereign LORD, you made the heavens and the earth by your great power and outstretched arm. Nothing is too hard for you' (*Jer.* 32:17). Similarly, in Acts 4, in equally difficult circumstances the apostles prayed, 'Sovereign Lord, you made the heaven and the earth and the sea, and everything in them' (verse 24).

What is it that persuaded them of the glory and greatness of God? It was the doctrine of creation.

Somebody once commented to me, 'Historically evangelicals have been strong on the doctrine of redemption and weak on the doctrine of creation.' I think that is true. But in Isaiah God is using this argument (from the nature of God's work as Creator) to persuade his people to trust him (as their Redeemer). Notice how he says: 'Do you not know? Have you not heard? Has it not been told you from the beginning? Have you not understood since the earth was founded?' (verse 21). Then he expounds to them how he created the heavens and the earth.

A. W. Pink is right when he says, 'The god of this century no more resembles the Sovereign of Holy Writ than does the dim flickering of a candle the glory of the midday sun.'[1] We need to

---

[1] Arthur W. Pink, *Gleanings in the Godhead* (Chicago: Moody Press, 1975), p. 28.

grasp that the God of Scripture is a God who holds the mountains in a balance and spans the universe with his hand. We get things in proper perspective when we see the uniqueness of God in creation.

INDEPENDENCE FROM THE CREATION

The second thing Isaiah turns to is the independence of God from the creation. Again he poses questions, this time to highlight the truth that ultimately the only totally independent being in the universe is God.

> Who has understood the Spirit of the LORD, or instructed him as his counsellor? Whom did the LORD consult to enlighten him, and who taught him the right way? Who was it that taught him knowledge or showed him the path of understanding? (verses 13–14).

One striking aspect of God's greatness is that he has no needs. Have you grasped this? 'Need' is a creature word. We have needs. God has none; he is complete in himself. His relationships with the rest of creation and with us as his people are a result of his sovereign will and pleasure, not because he has any need in himself or because he is incomplete without creating us.

I remember in my early days as a Christian attending a large meeting and hearing a missionary speaker. He told a harrowing story of a train crash that had taken place somewhere in the British Isles in which many people had been killed. Hundreds of badly injured persons were lying in the wreckage. From the train there emerged a man who was a fine surgeon. As he walked up and down among the injured people he was heard to say, 'If only I had my instruments . . .' He was helpless without them. After telling that story this missionary speaker pressed the moral upon us. 'That, my friends, is exactly what God is like in the world today. In the midst of the terrible crash that sin has brought, God walks up and down, saying, "If only I had my instruments."' I remember as a young man feeling sorry for God. I thought how frustrated he must be! Later in life I discovered that this was a distortion of the truth, not a representation of it. This is because the God of the Bible is complete in himself. He chooses to use us as his instruments, but he does not need to. His independence is an independence of mind, wisdom and purpose. He is the only utterly free agent in the universe.

Then again, God has no need of learning. He needs no teachers. All of us have teachers. None of us in the ultimate sense is original, although we like to think we are sometimes. We have all been taught. But when we ask, 'Who taught God his wisdom? From whom did he get understanding? Where did he earn his degrees?' the answer is, 'From no one.' God is the only untaught original mind. He is the only truly free agent. What God decrees, God does. What God decides, he performs. What God plans, he fulfils. Not only so, but his wisdom is perfect, unsullied and unspoiled by human imperfections. So his ways are perfect, his words are true, his decrees are good, his plans are flawless. And he never makes mistakes.

SUPREMACY ABOVE THE CREATION

The third thing Isaiah brings before us is God's supremacy over or pre-eminence above the creation. To establish the truth of the pre-eminence of God above creation Isaiah first turns to the nations of the earth. Compared to God, he says, they are like 'a drop in a bucket' (verse 15). We know how insignificant that is. As someone carries a bucket full of water, a drop may appear from the bottom and fall unnoticed to the earth. That is what the nations are like compared to God. Israel had become cowardly, being afraid of the power of the nations around them, and they had come to think of power in terms of human resources and influence. They needed to see that to God these things are like 'a drop in a bucket'.

Again, they are regarded as 'dust on the scales' (verse 15). When you are weighing most things, the dust on the scales is insignificant. The nations are like that to God. God weighs the islands as though they were fine dust.

Having demonstrated how lightweight and Lilliputian the nations are before God, in verse 16 Isaiah tells us that nothing man can offer to God in worship can ever adequately exalt or honour him. Lebanon is not sufficient for altar fires, nor its animals enough for burnt offerings. The vast cedar forests would not provide enough fuel for a proper altar on which to honour God, nor would its entire animal population be a sacrifice to present to him.

This is something we experience when we come to worship. In moments when we are brought into the presence of God and something of his infinite glory begins to warm our spirits, we recognize that we are totally incapable of offering God the worship that rightly belongs to him. No wonder Stephen Charnock says, 'It is in such an hour that the sensitive soul longs for heaven, because there we shall be free to worship, adore and honour him in the way that will truly magnify his name.'[1]

It is this infinite greatness of God which makes both images that represent God (verse 18) and idols which replace God (verses 19–20) so offensive to him.

To whom then will you compare God? What image will you compare him to?

That, of course, is the root of the second commandment: that we shall not make to ourselves any graven image. The greatness of God is inevitably going to be lessened and therefore blasphemed by making an image. In verses 19 and 20 Isaiah clarifies that for us, reaching at the end of verse 20 a moment of sarcasm in which he looks for a craftsman able to make an idol that will not topple over.

[1] Charnock, *op. cit.*, p. 239.

SOVEREIGNTY OVER THE CREATION

Fourth, Isaiah tells us that the greatness of God is revealed in his sovereignty over the creation (verses 21-24). Here again Isaiah wants to awaken the understanding of God's people.

> Do you not know? Have you not heard? Has it not been told you from the beginning? Have you not understood since the earth was founded? He sits enthroned above the circle of the earth, and its people are like grasshoppers (verses 21–22).

The prophet is charging the people with having forgotten the central fact of all life. That is, it is the living God who is on the throne both of heaven and earth. His greatness is exercised in his sovereign rule over everything he has made.

First, he is sovereign over the *earth:* 'He sits enthroned above the circle of the earth, and [before him] its people are like grasshoppers' (verse 22). But, of course, that is not how they thought of themselves. God's people were infected by a spirit of man-centredness, just as we are today. They were impressed by great men and had come to the conclusion that the course of history was decided by the princes and rulers of the earth. God sets their thinking straight: 'He brings princes to naught and reduces the rulers of this world to nothing' (verse 23). Why? Because it is he – and not they – who governs the affairs of the universe.

That is something we greatly need to learn in our generation. It is true, of course, that every period of history has produced its proud dictators, men who intend to establish kingdoms for themselves. But do you notice how Isaiah pictures them in verse 24?

> No sooner are they planted, no sooner are they sown, no sooner do they take root in the ground, than he blows on them and they wither, and a whirlwind sweeps them away like chaff (verse 24).

That is a vivid picture of the sovereign Lord ruling over all the nations of the earth.

Several years ago I stood in Munich, Germany, in one of the vast squares where Adolf Hitler once stood and addressed a multitude difficult to imagine as to size. But although the place is still there – it is a great area of open ground – Hitler and those who once stood with him are all gone. I thought of how he had once terrorized half the world and made the rest of the world tremble. But God blew on him, and he was swept away like chaff.

Do you remember Nikita Khrushchev, who ruled Russia when that country was putting its first space capsule into orbit? Khrushchev said, 'We are going up into space, and if we find God there, we will topple him from his throne.' But today many people have not even heard of Nikita Khrushchev! It is interesting to ask whose throne toppled first, is it not?

This is the kind of thing Isaiah was forcing people to think about, and we need to think about it today: especially today, when our vision of God has been so restricted that we have begun to get a man-centred view of the world and history. But the destinies of men and nations and the decisions that are going to affect the world in which we live are not taken in Washington, Moscow, London or any other human capital. They are taken where the Lord God omnipotent sits upon the throne of heaven. The government of the universe rests upon his shoulders, not ours. He is the God and Father of our Lord Jesus Christ, who in his mercy has become our Saviour. Our vision needs to be expanded to grasp that reality.

But notice, God is not only sovereign over the earth; he is sovereign over the *heavens* too.

'To whom will you compare me? Or who is my equal?' says the Holy One. Lift your eyes and look to the heavens: Who created all these? He who brings out the starry hosts one by one, and calls each of them by name.

For people who had been influenced by a Babylonian culture the significance of lifting one's eyes to the heavens was this: the Babylonians were devotees of astrology. They were primitive people who thought that their lives were ruled by stars. Have you ever come across other primitive people like that? I guess they opened their paper each morning to consult their horoscope to see whether it was propitious to do something on a particular day.

Do you know that in Britain today you can get all sorts of things through the telephone service? You can get 'Cricket Line', which gives you the scores of the latest cricket match. You can get 'Pop Line', which gives you ratings on pop music. You can get 'Story Line', which gives you a story any time of the day that you like to dial. Do you know the latest line? 'Star Line!' – it tells you your horoscope for the day. I was intrigued to read once in the London *Times* that it was the line with the heaviest use of all.

Well, these 'primitive' people believed that the stars controlled their destiny. But listen as Isaiah speaks the words God gave him.

> Lift your eyes and look to the heavens: Who created all these? He who brings out the starry hosts one by one, And calls each of them by name (verse 26).

The language is military. Isaiah is thinking of God as a general marching out the stars one by one. To us the stars are beyond numbering. But God summons each of the stars – every single one of them – by name. We know that there are as many stars as there are grains of sand on the seashore, but God has them all named. His greatness also extends to this, that he not only knows the stars by name but even has the hairs of the heads of his children numbered (*Matt.* 10:30).

God's greatness is related to his power over the stars of the universe. When he calls the stars to appear, not one of them is missing. Similarly, the eternal God is able thus to call out his people.

He knows them by name. And in the last day, because of his great power and strength, not one of *them* will be missing either.

HUMILITY AND HOPE

This leads directly to the application. If God can do that for the stars of the heavens, how much more will he do it for those who are his children?

There are two principal things which should be produced in the lives of God's people as a result of a new revelation of God's greatness. The first is genuine biblical humility. The second is genuine biblical hope.

Biblical humility is not something we affect. It is not a diffident personality. In fact, it is usually not something we are conscious of at all. It is simply a fruit of the knowledge of God, because nothing brings us to a true position of humility like a genuine vision of the eternal God and his greatness. When man begins to inflate and exalt himself in his stupidity, when he begins to imagine that he is possessed of some greatness in himself, what he desperately needs is an opening of his eyes to God's greatness.

But not only will this produce genuine biblical humility, it will also produce genuine biblical hope.

> Why do you say, O Jacob, and complain, O Israel, 'My way is hidden from the LORD; my cause is disregarded by my God?' ... (verse 27)

Here is a picture of a people beginning to lose hope, beginning to be overwhelmed by the weight of circumstances. Now, says Isaiah,

> Do you not know? Have you not heard? The LORD is the everlasting God, the Creator of the ends of the earth. He will not grow tired or weary, and his understanding no one can fathom. He gives strength to the weary and increases the power of the weak (verses 28–29).

Notice how greatness, strength and power do not depend on natural forces like youthfulness.

Even youths grow tired and weary, and young men stumble and fall; but those who hope in the LORD will renew their strength. They will soar on wings like eagles; they will run and not grow weary, they will walk and not faint (verses 30–31).

There is no greater illustration of that than the account in 2 Kings 6:8–23. It is my favourite story in the Old Testament. The king of Syria, Ben-Hadad, was distressed because the plans he had made to attack Israel were being communicated back to Israel's king. Thus whenever Ben-Hadad went out against Israel, the king of Israel knew where the attack would come, and the plans of Syria's king were frustrated.

So Ben-Hadad called his generals together and said, 'Something is going sadly wrong with our plans. Someone is revealing our plots to the king of Israel.'

They replied, 'That is not it at all, my lord. What is happening is that God is revealing our plans to the prophet Elisha in Dothan, and he is telling the king.'

'Get the army, send them down to Dothan, and capture the prophet', ordered the angry king.

The army of Syria and all the horses and chariots set out for Dothan to destroy Elisha. It is a fascinating picture, if you think of it. If somebody had stopped them on their journey and had said, 'Where is this huge army going and for what are you prepared?' they would have said: 'We are going to destroy the little prophet down in Dothan.' So much for so little! When they arrived they surrounded the city with their horses and chariots.

Elisha had one servant, a young man, who was probably in the school of the prophets. He heard the rumbling of the chariots and saw the mountainside filled with the horses and infantry of Ben-

Hadad. Trembling, he called to Elisha, 'Oh, my lord, what shall we do?' Elisha said, 'Don't be afraid. Those who are with us are more than those who are with them' (*2 Kings* 6: 16).

I can imagine the young man looking at the mountains, viewing the hosts of the enemy, looking at Elisha and himself and then, after listening to Elisha's voice, saying (no doubt to himself), 'That's the great problem with these old fellows. They are utterly unrealistic. They just do not face up to the facts of the contemporary situation.' But you see, it was the prophet who saw the facts clearly, not the young man. He turned to God and said, 'O LORD, open his eyes, so he may see.' And the Lord opened the young man's eyes, and he saw the mountain full of the horses and chariots of the Lord. That day God gained a glorious victory.

What is it that John says in his first epistle? 'The one who is in you is greater than the one who is in the world' (*1 John* 4:4). Of whom does John speak? If you turn to John 12:31, you will discover that 'the one who is in the world' is Satan. The One who casts him out is the Lord Jesus. So, the one who is in us and is greater than the one who is in the world is none other than the Lord Jesus Christ in his glory. Blessed be God for such a Saviour!

2

THE HOLINESS OF GOD

*I*T IS A SIMPLE, STATISTICAL FACT that 'holy' is the epithet applied to God more frequently in Scripture than any other. Jesus calls him 'holy Father' and teaches us to pray as our first request in the Lord's Prayer, 'Hallowed be your name' (*Matt.* 6:9).

Yet God's holiness is one of the most difficult concepts of all for us to understand. This is partly because of uncertainty – even the most accomplished linguists have it – about the derivation of the biblical words for 'holy'. It is also because holiness relates to God's very being. This is so much the case that it has been rightly said that to say that God is holy is just to say that God is God. Holiness belongs to the very essence of God's character. But, of course, the thing that makes it most difficult for us to conceptualize the holiness of God is that holiness relates to his distinctiveness. It is what makes God different from us. And it is because we are so remote from him in his holiness that we find it difficult to conceptualize this attribute.

Have you ever realized that we have the same problem in conceptualizing a perfectly holy God as we have in conceptualizing a wholly evil devil? It is because in both extremes we find that we are unable to conceptualize what is ultimate. In the case of God's character, we find it impossible to conceptualize his infinite holiness for the simple reason that we are sinners.

Nowhere is the meaning of holiness in God more fully expounded than in the teaching and preaching of Isaiah, and nowhere is

Isaiah's prophecy more helpful in this regard than in the great sixth chapter. Here, at the very outset of his ministry, Isaiah encounters God as the One whose essential nature is holiness.

Our purpose in studying this vision of God received by Isaiah is simply that, in some sense, our eyes also may be opened to see something of God's holiness.

There are two things that this passage sets before us: first, a *revelation* of God's holiness, and secondly, a *response* to God's holiness.

A REVELATION OF GOD'S HOLINESS

Three things about the revelation of God's holiness demand our attention.

First, *its timing*. It is obvious, isn't it, that for some reason Isaiah wanted to locate this vision in time? We are told at the beginning of chapter 6, 'In the year that King Uzziah died, I saw the Lord.' He is describing the exact period of time in which this occurred, so this must be of significance.

Uzziah's reign had been singularly beneficial to Judah. There had seldom been a king who sought the well-being of his people and did good for them, as Uzziah did. He was probably the greatest king since the days of Solomon. Yet in 2 Chronicles 26, we find that near the end of his reign Uzziah disparaged the glory of God, putting aside God's Word and counsel. Because of that the glory of God broke in upon him and he ended his days a leper. Uzziah has been called the king 'with that glorious reign with the ghastly end'.[1] So he became a great warning to others. He ended his life separated, cut off from the temple rather than being separated for it.

---

[1] George Adam Smith, *The Book of Isaiah* (London: Hodder and Stoughton, 1893), vol. 1, p. 59.

Significantly, it was in the year of the death of this man that Isaiah says he saw the Lord seated on a throne, high and exalted – a year when those who had put their trust in princes were finding their confidence shattered. By the very timing of the event, therefore, Isaiah highlights the vast distance between the greatest earthly monarch and the holy One of Israel.

Second, *the description*. It is not really clear whether Isaiah is describing the earthly or the heavenly temple in this vision. But the important thing is that he is seeing beyond the earthly temple to the heavenly one, noting that the glory of the Lord is filling it and dominating it. What dominates the temple, as Isaiah's vision begins, is the glory and presence of the Lord: 'I saw the Lord seated on a throne high, and exalted, and the train of his robe filled the temple.'

The word that is used for 'Lord' literally means 'the sovereign One'. This sovereign One is seated on a throne. Isaiah describes that throne as 'high and exalted'. In fact, by a peculiar combination in the Hebrew language, the words, 'high' and 'exalted', may qualify either 'sovereign Lord' or 'throne' or both. In Isaiah 57:15 God is shown as 'the high and lofty One . . . whose name is holy' who lives 'in a high and holy place'. But the picture here is of an exalted figure, the glorious King of the ages, whose holiness is manifested by his glory filling the temple. And it is, of course, God's holiness which exalts him above all he has made. He is transcendent, lifted up, separate from sinners, exalted.

But then, do you notice that when Isaiah begins to describe what he sees, his description of God goes no further than the train of his robe? 'In the year that King Uzziah died, I saw the Lord seated on a throne, high and exalted, and the train of his robe filled the temple.' That is a significant thing, because here Isaiah is discovering the very thing that we noted earlier: human language is an insufficient vehicle to describe God's holiness. So all Isaiah is able to say is, 'The train of his robe filled the temple.' It was, of course, the presence and glory of God which filled the temple, but Isaiah sees no further than the robe.

It is significant that, in the same way, in Exodus 24:10, when the elders of Israel saw God, all they have recorded is that the pavement under his feet was sapphire blue. They too found it impossible to describe God.

Ezekiel had the same problem. He begins to describe the glory of God, but he says, 'It was like unto the likeness of' something. He finds it impossible to grasp.

In this vision we are at the edge of an infinity of impossibility in understanding what the transcendent glory and holiness of God really is – so much does God's holiness separate him even from our imagination. John N. Oswalt says, 'There is a barrier beyond which the simply curious cannot penetrate.'[1]

Third, *the language*. Notice how God is described by the seraphic creatures we see in verses 2 and 3:

> Above him were seraphs, each with six wings: With two wings they covered their faces, with two they covered their feet, and with two they were flying. And they were calling to one another:
>
> 'Holy, holy, holy is the LORD Almighty;
> the whole earth is full of his glory.'

That key word, 'holy,' probably means 'separate, set apart, distinctive'. So, as it is applied to God, it denotes everything that is distinctive in God and which distinguishes God from his creation. The Old Testament concept of God's holiness, which is carried over into the New Testament, has to do essentially with God's moral glory and distinctiveness. It is important for us to grasp this, because the words 'holy' and 'holiness' are not in themselves

[1] *Isaiah* (New International Commentary), Zondervan, 1986, p. 178.

specifically Christian, religious or even Judaic. 'Holy' in Semitic usage refers simply to distinctiveness; even objects may become holy by belonging to God. But in biblical terms, the holiness of God is the distinctiveness that belongs to his moral glory. Therefore, it is an ethical concept.

Notice that the seraphim used this word 'holy' three times in succession: 'Holy, holy, holy is the LORD Almighty.' That needs explanation, because it is not repetition for the mere sake of rhythm or metre. The Hebrew language has no word for 'very'. Indeed, it has no forms corresponding to our English superlatives, like greatest, best, deepest, and so on. So Hebrew repeats the word. Thus, we find the Lord saying in the Aramaic language (which is related to Hebrew), 'Truly, truly I say to you.' It is a way of emphasizing that what he is saying is especially true and important. The repetition is a linguistic device to stress it. This is the only context in Scripture where a word is repeated three times. And it occurs only twice: here in Isaiah 6 and in Revelation 4:8, where the heavenly beings cry aloud to God in precisely this language:

'Holy, holy, holy is the Lord God Almighty,
who was, and is, and is to come.'

The emphasis teaches us that if there is one thing about God that is supremely important, it is his holiness: his moral glory, his distinctiveness from everything in his creation, and the perfection and beauty of his character. The seraphim raise the word 'holy' to the power of three, as it were, in order to press its significance upon us.

The other important word used by the seraphim is 'glory'. Do you notice the parallels? 'Holy, holy, holy is the LORD Almighty; the whole earth is full of his glory.' There is a balance of thought as well as a balance of language. It is between God's holiness and God's glory. That is an important thing, because the glory of God is really the outshining of all he is. The root meaning of the word 'glory' is 'weight' or 'heaviness'. Since the weight of something frequently reflects its worth, 'glory' came to mean that which gave something or someone honour or made him or it worthy of respect. That idea in the human realm, multiplied by infinity, gives some notion of what the glory of God is. It is all that makes him worthy of praise in heaven as well as on earth.

GOD'S GLORY REVEALED

God reveals his glory in various ways. He has done it in creation: 'The heavens declare the glory of God' (*Psa.* 19:1), 'The whole earth is full of his glory' (*Isa.* 6:3). Supremely, of course, God has manifested his glory in the face of Jesus Christ. John wrote, 'We have seen his glory, the glory of the one and only Son, who came from the Father, full of grace and truth' (*John* 1:14).

Jesus is the express image of God's glory, and men and women saw his glory veiled in flesh during the incarnation. It was carefully veiled, but now and again it broke through.

Do you remember how on the Mount of Transfiguration there was that glorious moment when Peter, James and John saw something they could neither understand nor describe? The Lord began to shine like the sun. His raiment was white, in a way that no launderer could whiten it. What was happening was that something of the fullness of his glory, which was hidden by his flesh, broke through, and they found themselves bowed down in wonder. Later they said, 'We were eyewitnesses of his majesty' (*2 Pet.* 1:16). This is the glory the Lord is pleading for in John 17: 'And now, Father, glorify me in your presence with the glory I had with you before the world began' (verse 5).

There is another place where God manifests his glory. It is in the lives of his people. Do you remember what Jesus says in his great high priestly prayer? 'I have given them the glory that you gave me' (verse 22). Or again, as the Apostle Paul says, using the word used of the transformation of Christ on the mountain, the word 'metamorphosed', 'We . . . are being transformed into his likeness with ever-increasing glory, which comes from the Lord' (*2 Cor.* 3:18). God's design is to manifest his glory, not only in the heavens, in the created order, and in the face of Jesus Christ, but in the lives of his redeemed people.

A RESPONSE TO GOD'S HOLINESS

The response to God's holiness found in Isaiah 6 is seen in the three spheres of God's creation:

1. *The unfallen creation*, the seraphim (they were creatures, but they were unfallen creatures).

2. *The non-rational creation* (at the sound of the seraphim's voices the doorposts and threshold shook, and the temple was filled with smoke).

3. *The fallen creation*, represented by Isaiah himself, who cries, 'Woe to me! . . . I am ruined!'

First, *the unfallen creation*. The seraphim typify the right and appropriate response of creation to God's holiness. George Adam Smith says they are, 'all wings and voice. Perfect readinesses of praise and service.'[1]

Notice how their wings are employed. One pair of wings covered their faces. Even the unfallen creation cannot gaze on the holiness of God uncovered. The sight would in some sense be more than even the unfallen creation could bear. 'No more', says Adam Smith, 'could one gaze at the sun than they could gaze at God.'[2] So

[1] *Isaiah*, p. 63.
[2] Quoted by R. A. Finlayson, *The Holiness of God* (London: Westminster Chapel Bookroom, 1955), p. 11.

they cover their faces for their own sake, because they cannot bear this burning glory, which is the holiness of God.

Another pair of wings covered their feet. Professor E. J. Young thinks this is a gesture of humility and self-abasing modesty, and I think he is right. They are recognizing that in the presence of the holiness of God, they need some moral covering.

The third pair of wings is employed in enabling them to be swift in the glad service of such a glorious God.

Notice also that they cry *to one another*. This is an important element, because it shows us that their response to an experience of God's holiness is not non-rational. On the contrary, their minds are engaged in the task of communicating with one another about the holiness and glory of God. They are actually speaking to one another and mutually encouraging one another to glory in God cognitively, rationally and verbally. There is a lesson for us here: namely, that no rational being can employ his mind more fully than in speaking about the glory of God and about his holiness. In this exercise, our mental processes will always be employed to the fullest possible extent.

Their experience of the holiness of God brought the seraphim to communicate with one another in what, I suppose, was their deepest and most godly fellowship. Isn't this what we are doing when we are engaging in true fellowship? True fellowship is not coffee and biscuits after the evening service. True fellowship is glorying in our Redeemer. It is sharing in the wonder of all that God is. We do that in some of our hymns. The psalmist does it: 'Glorify the LORD with me; let us exalt his name together' (*Psa.* 34:3). Of course, there is no reason why you cannot do this while having coffee and biscuits after the service. But what is of immense importance to grasp is that true biblical fellowship is exulting in the one thing we have in common, and that is the glory of our great God and Saviour. That is what these angelic beings were doing. Therefore, we see that the most profound, moving and uplifting experience of the holiness of God has a rational core to it.

Second, *the non-rational creation*. In verse 4, the whole temple building is affected by the presence of the Holy One. At the sound of the voices that were magnifying God's holiness, the doorposts and thresholds shook. The reason for that was, of course, that the very foundations of the temple were being moved. The earth beneath Isaiah's feet was trembling. Do you see what is happening? If the created beings God has made to worship him will not tremble, then the inanimate creation trembles. The whole earth quivers and itself speaks of the terribleness of God's holiness.

Third, *the fallen creation*. It responds in verse 5. The unfallen beings, as we saw, cover their faces and feet and fly to do God's bidding. The non-rational creation trembles and shakes in God's presence. But notice: the fallen creation, represented by Isaiah personally, cries out in despair and distress. 'Woe to me! . . . I am ruined! For I am a man of unclean lips, and I live among a people of unclean lips, and my eyes have seen the King, the LORD Almighty.'

If we look to the previous chapter, we will find that Isaiah had been reviewing the sins of his people. He had been sent to pronounce judgment on them. For example, in verse 18, he cried out, 'Woe to those who draw sin along with cords of deceit, and wickedness as with cart ropes.' In verse 20 he wrote, 'Woe to those who call evil good and good evil.' Verse 21 says, 'Woe to those who are wise in their own eyes.' Verse 22: 'Woe to those who are heroes at drinking wine and champions at mixing drinks, who acquit the guilty for a bribe, but deny justice to the innocent.' In this chapter Isaiah is pronouncing woes upon all sorts of sin in society.

But notice that when he is faced with the Holy One himself all he can say is, 'Woe to me! I am ruined! I am finished! I am without hope!' The man is in consternation of spirit and deep distress of soul. Why? There is one overwhelming reason for this state of distress and conviction, and that is the defilement of his own sin which he is aware of when he is brought into the presence of the burning holiness of God.

At first we might be inclined to regard Isaiah's distress as exaggerated, because it is concentrated on something that we would regard as perhaps an amiable weakness rather than a desperate cause of brokenness before God: his 'unclean lips'. Unclean lips do not seem to us to be the sort of things that should cause the distress Isaiah here experiences. But his distress over even this highlights the utter horror of sin as seen in the presence of the holiness of God. That is what makes the difference.

Oswald Sanders, General Director of the old China Inland Mission, once wrote: 'When one reads of the Puritans mourning over their sin, one can only conclude that either they were very wicked men or we are very superficial Christians.'[1]

Do you know the words spoken by Quasimodo in Victor Hugo's famous book, *The Hunchback of Notre Dame*? He takes a beautiful young woman up into the tower of Notre Dame. And there, as he looks at her face, he says, 'I never realized how ugly I was until I saw your beauty.' It is like that with God. It is seeing him in his holiness that produces conviction of sin. That is what causes us to cry out, 'I am a man of unclean lips, and I live among a people of unclean lips.'

CLEANSED AND TRANSFORMED

Isaiah's experience of God's holiness had another and more wonderful dimension to it. He had found that God displays his holiness in order that men and angels may stand in awe of him as the Holy

---

[1] Oswald Sanders, *Men from God's School* (London: Marshall, Morgan & Scott, 1965), p. 146.

One. But God now turns his attention to his fallen creature so that this servant of his may begin to know the cleansing, transforming touch of the same God who has crushed him to the ground. It is so that he might be a partaker of that holiness.

There are many of God's attributes that we will never share. Theologians call them his 'incommunicable attributes' – his omnipotence, for example. God does not share his omnipotence. His omniscience also. God does not share his knowledge of all things with us.

But there is a daring and glorious word in Hebrews 12, which tells us that God has planned for us to be partakers of his holiness: 'God disciplines us for our good, that we may share in his holiness' (verse 10). Here, in Isaiah 6, we get an adumbration of what God was yet to do in Jesus Christ to make atonement for sin, in order that he might take a man like Isaiah and reproduce his holiness in him. So we find one of the seraphim, who have been shy of the holiness of God, nevertheless flying to the altar of God – that is, to the place of atonement – where he takes a live coal and then lays it on Isaiah's lips, the place where he was most conscious of his sin. And then the gospel is preached to Isaiah! 'See, this has touched your lips; your guilt is taken away and your sin is atoned for' (verse 7).

What is happening? Some people have imagined that it was a charred piece of the burnt offering that was taken from the altar and applied to Isaiah's lips. But whatever was happening, whether this or something else, it was a work of cleansing, coming from the altar of atonement. Why was God ministering his atoning mercy to his sin-stricken servant? He was preparing him to be a man in whose life he would manifest his holiness.

Of course, Isaiah 6:6 and 7 is only a prophetic glimpse of the supreme place where God was to bring his holiness and mercy together, namely, at the cross of Jesus Christ. Again the earth trembled. The sun was darkened. But this time it was the Lord who cried out, 'Woe to me! I am undone! My God, my God, why have you forsaken me?' By that sacrifice, God was procuring for us a redemption designed to restore God's glory in God's creatures and, wonder of wonders, enable us to become bearers of his holiness.

3

THE SOVEREIGNTY OF GOD

E TURN NOW TO CONSIDER the sovereignty of God, and especially to see how this truth is wonderfully expounded in Acts 4:23–31.

Peter and John have been put in prison and released. The narrative continues:

> On their release, Peter and John went back to their own people and reported all that the chief priests and elders had said to them. When they heard this, they raised their voices together in prayer to God. 'Sovereign Lord,' they said 'You made the heaven and the earth and the sea, and everything in them. You spoke by the Holy Spirit through the mouth of your servant, our father David:
>
> Why do the nations rage
> and the peoples plot in vain?
> The kings of the earth take their stand
> and the rulers gather together against the Lord
> and against his Anointed One.
>
> Indeed Herod and Pontius Pilate met together with the Gentiles and the people of Israel in this city to conspire against your holy servant Jesus, whom you anointed.
> They did what your power and will had decided beforehand should happen. Now, Lord, consider their threats and enable your servants to speak your word with great boldness. Stretch

out your hand to heal, and perform miraculous signs and wonders through the name of your holy servant, Jesus.'

After they prayed, the place where they were meeting was shaken, and they were all filled with the Holy Spirit and spoke the word of God boldly (*Acts* 4:23–31).

Most of that passage is a prayer. It is the first recorded prayer of the early church, and it was provoked by the first major crisis the new community had faced. Peter and John had been imprisoned and warned, as they were set free, that they must never again speak in the name of Jesus (verse 18). This was a threat to the continued expansion of the gospel. So, on their release, Peter and John went back to their people and reported all that the chief priests and elders had said.

They give themselves to prayer at that point, and the substance of their prayer is what someone has described as the underlying conviction of the whole Bible: namely, that God is the sovereign King who reigns as Lord over the whole universe. God is living and active. He has not abdicated his throne. His reign is therefore effectual and absolute. He exercises sovereign control over history.

The conviction that God is on the throne and is overruling even the wrath of his enemies was an important thing for the early church to be assured of at this moment. But it is at least equally vital for the contemporary church. In today's world there is a persistent question which, as Francis Schaeffer used to say, 'grumbles under the skin of every thinking man.' To whom does ultimate power belong? Or perhaps: Is there a controlling hand on history? Is there some sovereign power that actually directs the affairs of men and nations on this planet?

We need the assurance the apostles and the early church had. We need to be assured that the God we have come to know through Jesus Christ really does cause all things to work together for good to those who love him and that he really is sovereign – not only over history in general but over our personal histories too.

These crucial questions are answered in the two words by which the early Christians addressed God in this prayer: 'Sovereign Lord.' These words are crucial, for the rest of the prayer is only an expansion of the conviction expressed in them.

Notice that the early believers addressed God in four ways.

They addressed God, first, as *the sovereign Lord of creation:* 'Sovereign Lord,' they said, 'you made the heaven and the earth and the sea, and everything in them' (verse 24).

Second, they addressed God as *the sovereign Lord of history:* 'You spoke by the Holy Spirit through the mouth of your servant, our father David:

"Why do the nations rage
and the peoples plot in vain?
The kings of the earth take their stand
and the rulers gather together against the Lord
and against His anointed One"' (verses 25, 26).

Third, they addressed God as *the sovereign Lord of redemption:* 'Indeed Herod and Pontius Pilate met together with the Gentiles and the people of Israel in this city to conspire against your holy servant Jesus, whom you anointed. They did what your power and will had decided beforehand should happen' (verses 27, 28).

Fourth, they spoke to God as *the sovereign Lord of the contemporary scene:* 'Now, Lord, consider their threats and enable your servants to speak your word with great boldness' (verse 29).

We need to work over these and look at each of them a bit more fully.

LORD OF CREATION

It is a significant thing that these early believers rightly recognized that the place where the doctrine of God's sovereignty is first revealed in Scripture is in the first chapter of Genesis. There we have a magnificent picture of God, sitting upon the throne of the universe issuing verbal decrees. 'Let there be', he says. He repeats it again and again. And after every decree there comes the expression, 'And it was so.' Nothing could be more sovereign than the simple speaking of a commandment which is thus instantly obeyed.

The entire created order – 'the heaven and the earth and the sea, and everything in them' – owes its origin to the sovereign decree of God as King of the universe, sitting upon his throne.

This means that the decision to create is entirely God's. And in the act of creation, God acts in total freedom – an illustration of the fact that God is the only totally free Spirit. He acts in freedom as he issues his decrees, calling into being all that is.

As it left the hand of God, the creation was, so to speak, an expression of the sovereign will of God and reflected the perfect order of God's mind. It was all very good because it was the result of God's sovereign activity.

It is this which guarantees the rationality of the universe and makes scientific research possible. But the significance of it for the apostles was that it persuaded them to trust God for their present situation.

It is sometimes said that the doctrine of God's sovereignty poses a problem in that it makes prayer unnecessary. People say, 'Why should we pray if God in his sovereignty overrules everything that is going to happen? If every detail is under his sovereign control, is not prayer meaningless?' But God's sovereignty makes prayer possible, not unnecessary. That is why, as the apostles pray, they remind themselves of God's sovereign power in creation.

The argument from God's sovereignty in creation is used in two ways in the Bible. It is used, on the one hand, *by men as they plead with God.* Here is an area in which the sovereignty of God becomes a ground on which God's people stand as they plead with him. Listen to Jeremiah 32:17: 'Ah, Sovereign LORD [it is the same expression], you have made the heavens and the earth by your great power and outstretched arm. Nothing is too hard for you.' What empowers Jeremiah in that prayer, what gives ground to him in pleading with God and, as it were, reasoning with God, is his recalling the sovereign power of God, who had but to speak and the universe was called into being.

We also find this conviction used *by God to persuade men to trust him.* For example, in Isaiah 40 we find God's people in the same kind of condition in which they are so often found today: fearful, apologetic, defensive and distrustful of God. But when God finds them in that condition, what does he say to them? He reminds them of the doctrine of his sovereignty in creation.

'To whom will you compare me? Or who is my equal?' says the Holy One. Lift your eyes and look to the heavens: Who created all these? . . . Do you not know? Have you not heard? The LORD is the everlasting God, the Creator of the ends of the earth?

Therefore,

Those who hope in the LORD will renew their strength. They will soar on wings like eagles; they will run and not grow weary, they will walk and not faint (*Isa.* 40:25, 26, 28, 31).

We need some of that spirit ourselves these days. We need to catch a picture of the sovereign majesty of God, who commands and it is done.

Genesis 1 tells us that God made this and that. He created the heavens and the earth. Then we get the greatest throwaway line

35

in all literature: 'He also made the stars' (verse 16). Beautiful! But if God is able to do all this, then we must understand that it is surely the cure for the problem that our God is too small. Where do we get a vision of God in his majesty? It is in creation. No wonder people are trying to rob us of the doctrine of creation. What they are trying to do is not a scientific matter; it is a spiritual matter.

So the apostles were right to begin their prayer by saying, 'Sovereign Lord, you made the heavens and the earth and the sea, and everything in them.'

LORD OF HISTORY

Second, they address him as *the sovereign Lord of history*. Verses 25 and 26 are a quotation from Psalm 2 – a Psalm of which the German Old Testament scholar, Artur Weiser, wrote:

> It is to this God that the psalm bears witness, characterizing him as a God who is present and active, who knows how to make himself respected by those who do not want to give heed to him, and who accomplishes his purpose even though men rebel against him.[1]

The immediate context of Psalm 2 is the accession and anointing of a new king, who has been chosen by God. The kings of the earth stage a rebellion against him. That is the theme of the earlier part of the Psalm.

> Why do the nations rage
> and the peoples plot in vain?
> The kings of the earth take their stand
> and the rulers gather together against the LORD
> and against his Anointed One (verses 1, 2).

[1] A. Weiser, *The Psalms* trans. H. Hartwell (London: S.C.M. Press, 1962), p. 112.

From the psalmist's point of view, the very idea of mere man staging a rebellion against the sovereign Lord of all men and nations is ludicrous. It is like mice attempting to challenge a lion. So he says, 'The One enthroned in heaven laughs.' He rebukes them, saying,

I have installed my King
on Zion, my holy hill (verse 6).

What God is doing in those verses is asserting his sovereignty over the historical process. He raises up kings and casts down authorities. He has the last word in history, and he is mocking these nations who seek to rebel against him, thinking they have sovereignty instead of God.

Weiser again puts his finger on the issue here:

At the centre of history is no longer the struggle of the great world powers for existence, but God, whose relationship with the earthly powers will determine their destiny.[1]

His vision of history (this is of cardinal importance) is theocentric. A true view of God's sovereignty should make history theocentric for us too. We should see that God is at the centre and that the real decisions are not being taken in Beijing, New York, London, or wherever. Rather, the decisions that will ultimately determine the consummation of human history are being taken at the throne of God. It is because the government rests upon his shoulders – not upon the shoulders of any man or combination of men and women – that this is done.

Do you really believe that? Is that the central conviction of your life about history? Those of us who preach sometimes speak about ministering with our Bibles in one hand and our newspapers in the other. The truth that should focus our understanding of current affairs is that there is a living God who is on the throne

[1] Weiser, *The Psalms*, p. III.

of his universe. History is not circular. It is not going round in meaningless cycles. History is linear. It is moving towards that great and awesome day when our Lord Jesus Christ will return in glory, when God will pull down the curtain on history and declare that this bankrupt world must be brought to the last assize. That is the view of history that a sovereign Lord, sitting on the throne, gives to us.

This needs to be seen in light of the other attributes of God. One of the most dangerous things one can do is to set some of the attributes of God against others. God's sovereignty, for example, is never exercised so as to be inconsistent with his holiness, righteousness, goodness, justice, and so on. God may even use the wrath of men to praise him.

So when you see people cynically imagining that they have the last word on some situation – that by political cunning or devious means they have achieved some kind of temporary victory – we ought not to tremble but to shake our heads and say, 'Poor, deluded fool. He does not know that the eternal God, who is sitting on the throne, is able to take him up and cast him aside, even with the breath of his lips.'

Do you remember how Joseph expressed this in Genesis 50? After his father died, the brothers who sold him into slavery came to him, desperately wanting to know he really forgave them. He said to them, 'You intended to harm me, but God intended it for good' (verse 20). According to Joseph, even the foul deceit, disloyalty and cunning of his brothers were unable to deflect the sovereign purposes of God for his and others' history. God is never caught unprepared; he is never baffled.

LORD OF REDEMPTION

Third, having addressed God as the sovereign Lord of creation and of history, the disciples next address him as *the sovereign Lord of redemption.* This follows from their citation of Psalm 2, for they clearly saw this Psalm as messianic. The rulers of their day had certainly conspired 'against the Lord and against his Anointed One'. But the great watershed of history and, therefore, the greatest display of God's sovereign power in history was the redemption he accomplished in Jesus Christ in spite of man's rebellion against him. Here, more than anywhere, God turned the wrath of men to praise him.

The apostles saw the ultimate fulfilment of what Psalm 2 was describing on the day Christ was crucified outside Jerusalem. But in that day, when the land became dark, God was the one wielding real power and authority.

We can see the special significance of that to them personally, since they were living in a moment when the powers of darkness were gathered together to silence them as witnesses to this same Jesus. They looked back, asking, 'Whose hand was in control of the situation when Jesus was being taken by Herod and Pontius Pilate and they, together with the Gentiles and the people of Israel, were about to crucify him? Who was in ultimate control of everything that was happening? It was our God, of course.' Listen to what they actually did say: 'They did what your power and your will had decided beforehand should happen.'

Pilate had such delusions of grandeur. Do you remember when he had the silent Jesus before him and asked, 'Do you refuse to speak to me? Do you not realize who I am? Don't you realize I have power either to free you or to crucify you? Do you not realize that you are in the presence of great authority and power? Can you not see this?'

Jesus said to him, 'You would have no power over me if it were not given to you from above' (*John* 19:8–11).

That is one of the greatest statements of the sovereignty of God in the Bible. Jesus was apparently a helpless prisoner, subject to the power of the Roman Empire, but he said to Pilate, 'You would have no power at all except it were given to you by my Father.' In other words, the real decisions had already been made – by God, not by man! Pilate, Herod, the Gentiles and the people of Israel were mere instruments in the hand of a sovereign God, who was accomplishing *his* rather than *their* purpose. They did not think that, of course. That would have been a most ludicrous idea to them. But that was actually what was happening.

We too have misunderstandings about some of these great decisions. I remember Charles Colson saying that, when he worked in the White House, Henry Kissinger used to come in every day and say with a great sense of melodrama, 'Mr President, we have been making decisions today which are going to alter the course of history.' Colson said that Kissinger was always altering the course of history – almost every day. He had a sense of grandeur in the decisions they were making. But the things that really matter in human history have already been decided by the living, eternal God, who sits on the throne of the universe and will never abdicate it. He has taken decisions that are going to be worked out inexorably. And nothing will hinder him. Nothing! Even the wrath of nations becomes an instrument in his hand.

It is in this sense that Jesus is described as 'the Lamb that was slain from the creation of the world' (*Rev.* 13:8). God is so absolutely sovereign in the achievement of our salvation that he had planned it before time began, accomplished it at the time of his choosing, and is now taking it on to its consummation at the return of Christ.

Scripture also tells us that God is sovereign in the application of redemption because, as Jesus said, 'No-one can come to me unless the Father who sent me draws him' (*John* 6:44).

The result – the new creation in Christ – is just as clearly a work of God's sovereign power as the old creation. Regeneration is a sovereign work of God; repentance is a sovereign gift of God. So is faith. It is of vital importance for us to grasp that, if for no other reason than that we need to recognize to whom we apply for a work of this kind.

When we are considering the question of the application of God's redeeming grace to the lives of men and women, to whom do we primarily apply for it? Well, even in evangelism there are certain things we are able to do ourselves. We may try to persuade sinners of certain truths. We may move them. We may stir them emotionally. But when we are talking about regenerating them spiritually, that is a work of the sovereign power of God. We have no more to do with our own spiritual birth than we have to do with our physical birth. It is of God.

The implication of this is obvious, isn't it? It concerns the primary evangelistic method, which is prayer. That is as clear as day following night. It is logically irrefutable. But the church is crippled in our modern world because, although we believe this with our heads, we do not put it into practice. It does not affect our priorities. We would have a different view of prayer if we really believed that from its conception in eternity to its consummation at Christ's return, salvation is the work of God's sovereign grace.

LORD OF THE CONTEMPORARY SCENE

Finally, the disciples address God as *Lord of the contemporary scene*. Look at verse 29: 'Now, Lord, consider their threats and enable your servants to speak your word with great boldness.' Having reviewed God's sovereignty in creation, history and redemption, they turn to the present. And, obviously the whole point of their contemplating the truth of God's sovereignty in those three spheres is that they might apply the truth to their own situation.

This was not merely an academic exercise. They needed to clarify their minds and strengthen their souls by this truth. So they are reminding themselves that the God of whom they have been thinking is not the great 'I was' but the great 'I am'. He is still like this. He is precisely the same God who decreed light to shine out of darkness, who sovereignly overrules history and who directed in grace the events leading to the death and resurrection of Jesus Christ. 'Therefore,' they say, 'we entrust this present situation to you.'

You will notice that they seek God's power not for their own protection primarily, but in the interests of evangelism. They are concerned for bold proclamation of the gospel. They say, 'Enable your servants to speak your word with great boldness.' It is the sovereign power of God alone that will enable them to do this. There is an extraordinary idea in some places that there is a conflict between the sovereignty of God and evangelistic zeal. But the two are friends not enemies. The one ought to flow out of the other.

TWO VALUABLE RESULTS

There are two things that the conviction about God's sovereignty did for the apostles. It gave them *biblical humility:* 'Now, Lord, consider their threats and enable your servants . . .' (*Acts* 4:29). This is the language of people who know that they have no power or authority (indeed, nothing) of themselves, but are utterly dependent upon God.

Humility is a very difficult thing for us to speak about, isn't it? We tend to think of it rather in human terms or in terms that come out of our readings in literature. In Charles Dickens' great novel *David Copperfield* there is a character whose name is Uriah Heap. He is the quintessential humble man. He says, 'I'm just a humble man, Mr Copperfield, just a humble, ordinary man.' But he is not, of course. (The great way, incidentally, to puncture that kind of humility, is to agree with it, saying, 'Yes, you are just an ordinary, little man, with no significance at all.' That is how you find out whether humility is real or not!) That grovelling, self-abasing attitude is not biblical humility. True humility is something of which the man who possesses it is totally unaware.

The sovereignty of God is the soil in which biblical humility grows. That is why the Reformed faith creates character, when it is rightly applied. It produces godly lowliness and meekness of mind because it recognizes that everything we are and anything good that can ever appear in us is the gift of a sovereign God. So biblical humility is the first fruit of a true appreciation of God's sovereignty.

The second result is *spiritual energy*. Notice what the disciples wanted God's help for. They wanted it for preaching and teaching the Word of God with boldness. And that is what happened. After they had prayed, the place where they were meeting was shaken. They were all filled with the Holy Spirit, and they spoke the Word of God boldly. We need that spiritual energy desperately in our day. It is a very significant thing, I think, that these disciples knew the reality of it when they were preoccupied, not with themselves or with anything else, but with God in his sovereignty.

I remember – as a very young Christian – hearing Duncan Campbell, who had come down from the revival on the Isle of Lewis in Scotland in the early 1950s. He spoke about that revival and said to us, 'Ultimately, I am bound to say to you, my dear friends, that the one thing that I have been aware of in Lewis over these last months is that at the centre of everything, there is the living God, exalted in his sovereign glory.'

We need this same theocentric vision. Our problem is that so much of our Christian thinking is anthropocentric rather than theocentric. May God give us the right vision and focus our minds to see all things in his perspective.

4

THE FAITHFULNESS OF GOD

*I*T IS A SIGNIFICANT COMMENT on the pattern of modern life that the most common way in which the word 'faithfulness' occurs on our lips is with the negative prefix *un:* 'unfaithfulness'. In the *commercial* world, a man's word is seldom his bond any more. We have experienced this in an acute form in the commercial life of the great financial centres of the western world, because nobody is able to trust anybody else any longer. In the *domestic* world, strict marital fidelity is regarded as a quaint curiosity. In the *ecclesiastical* and *theological* realm, faithfulness to the written Word of God, the apostolic gospel, and the confessional standards of the church to which we have committed ourselves are dismissed as narrow-minded obscurantism.

The reason for all this, of course, is the unreliability of human nature. This is why the psalmist urges us not to put our trust in princes, nor in men who are mortal (*Psa.* 146:3). Rather, we are to ponder the divine nature and rest in the character of God. Scripture speaks in superlative terms about God's faithfulness: 'Your faithfulness [reaches] to the skies,' says Psalm 36:5; 'Your faithfulness continues through all generations,' says Psalm 119:90; 'Great is your faithfulness,' says the writer of Lamentations (3:23).

Faithfulness is an aspect of the perfection of God's character. God is utterly reliable. Therefore, there never has been a promise that God has made that he will not fulfil in detail. There is no covenant that he has entered into that he will not make good.

Balaam urges Balak to recognize the difference between divine and human nature, saying, 'God is not a man, that he should lie, nor a son of man, that he should change his mind. Does he speak and then not act? Does he promise and not fulfil?' (*Num.* 23:19). The questions are couched in such terms that everything in the universe cries out, 'What God says, he will do. What he promises, he will fulfil.'

The eighty-ninth Psalm is full of this theme. It is divided into two parts. Verses 1 to 37, the longer first section, are a celebration and exposition of God's faithfulness. The theme is set in verse 1: 'With my mouth I will make your faithfulness known through all generations.' The second part, verse 38 to the end of the Psalm, presents a contrast. These verses are not a celebration; they are a complaint against God: that he appears to have made his faithfulness invisible. His frowning providence seems to be denying it. The psalmist says:

> You have rejected, you have spurned, you have been very angry with your anointed one. You have renounced the covenant with your servant and defiled his crown in the dust (verses 38, 39).

He cries out in verse 49,

> O Lord, where is your former great love, which in your faithfulness you swore to David?

As we approach these words, it is important to remember that, as in many of the Psalms, the beginning of the Psalm is actually the conclusion that the psalmist has reached, having gone through the anguish of spirit which he later describes.

Alexander Maclaren says that the unique thing about Psalm 89 is that 'this bird can sing in midwinter'.[1] When there is winter in

---

[1] A. Maclaren, *The Psalms* (London: Hodder and Stoughton, 1896), vol. 2, p. 491.

his soul, the psalmist is still able to cry aloud of the Lord's great faithfulness.

FAITHFUL IN HIS NATURE

As he sings of the faithfulness of God, the psalmist tells us several important things about it.

First, God is faithful in his nature; that is, in his very constitution, God is faithful. It is his great characteristic, now and 'through all generations' (verse 1).

From verse 5 on, we are led into the heavens where God's faithfulness is praised in the assembly of the holy ones. 'Holy ones' refers to the angelic host surrounding God, who are nearest to him, and are, therefore, best able to observe his nature. You know how we say that when you live with somebody, that is when you really get to know them. I have heard people say that about the person they have married: 'I didn't really know him (or her) until I lived with him.' Well, the angelic host live in close communion with God, and they are able to observe him.

'What then, do they celebrate about him in heaven?' asks the psalmist. The answer is: 'God's faithfulness.'

The psalmist compares God with the unfallen creation, asking,

Who in the skies above can compare with the LORD?
Who is like the LORD among the heavenly beings? (verse 6).

And what is the point of comparison?

You are mighty, O LORD, and your *faithfulness* surrounds you (verse 8).

Verse 37 says that the line of David will be established forever like the moon, the faithful witness in the sky.

The heavenly bodies are witnesses to the unchanging consistency that is in God. He is the one unchanging feature of the universe, around which all else is quicksand. There is in God's nature a constancy which makes him utterly reliable.

You will remember the reason Paul gives in 2 Timothy 2:13 to explain why God remains faithful, even if we are faithless. It is that 'he cannot deny himself'. Similarly, to Titus he says, 'God . . . cannot lie' (*Titus* 1:2, KJV). God cannot be untrue to himself. Since he is faithful, he cannot lie.

In Hebrew the word for 'faithfulness' has the same root as the word 'Amen.' So when we say 'Amen' to something, we are saying, 'That is true. It is a faithful saying.' In light of this, it is interesting that in Revelation, when the Lord Jesus Christ is being spoken of, he is introduced as 'the Amen, the faithful and true witness' (*Rev.* 3:14). This is his essence, in other words. Faithfulness is God's nature. Time does not change him, as it changes us. Nor do moods change God, as they change us.

You know how it is with people. At work someone will say, 'How are we going to find the boss today? What sort of weekend will he have had? Has he had a difficult time with his family? If so, it is going to make it difficult for us. I wonder if he will be the same as he was on Friday?' One of the problems we have is that we imagine God being like the people we see around us – fluctuating, different, changed by moods, health, stress and provocation. But Psalm 102:27 says, 'You remain the same.' All else may change, but God is constant.

Again, because God is faithful in his nature, he never does anything out of character. We do things out of character, and so do other people.

As a minor part of my work as a minister I served as chaplain to the High Court in Glasgow. I sat there frequently, listening to some of the pleas of some of the best defence lawyers in Scotland. They would say to the judge, 'But, my Lord, what the defendant did was quite out of character. It denied all that he really is. You must listen to me as I tell you what the man is really like.' It may have been so. Or it may not! But we never have to say that of God. Throughout eternity God has never acted inconsistently with himself. There has never been an occasion when God has done anything even the least degree out of character.

We may apply that to our own experience. In all his dealings with me, even when it is winter in my soul, I am able to sing of the faithfulness of God. I can do that because I know that God will never do anything out of step with his true nature. He 'does not change like shifting shadows', says James (1:17).

FAITHFUL IN HIS LOVE

The psalmist also tells us that God is faithful in his love. You can tell a lot about words in the Bible by the company they keep, and in Psalm 89, we find God's faithfulness and God's steadfast love brought together. They seem to have a special relationship. Look at these examples:

> I will sing of the Lord's great *love* forever;
> with my mouth I will make your *faithfulness* known (verse 1).

> I will declare that your *love* stands firm forever,
> that you established your *faithfulness* in heaven itself (verse 2).

> Righteousness and justice are the foundation of your throne;
> *love* and *faithfulness* go before you (verse 14).

> My *faithful love* will be with him (verse 24).

> I will not take my *love* from him,
> nor will I ever betray my *faithfulness* (verse 33).

The point is that God's love stands firm. There is no place where he displays his faithfulness more truly than in what the Bible calls his 'covenant love'. Covenant love is the proper translation of one particularly strong Hebrew word for love – 'steadfast love', as some of the versions translate it. Covenant love is love that never changes, because it is unconditional and unconditioned. It finds no stimulus outside of God to create it, and it finds no influence which can alter it in any way.

In verse 3, the psalmist sees this love of God expressed in the covenant he made with David – a reference to 2 Samuel 7. In fact the Bible is full of God's saving covenant. God comes to us with something like a marriage proposal: 'I will be your God; you will be my people. I will bless and keep you.'

It is interesting that in marriage, we ourselves speak about an unconditional covenant, not a covenant that is conditioned. For example, when I have two people before me in church and am about to marry them, I use the language of the covenant. I ask the bridegroom, 'Do you promise and covenant in the presence of Almighty God and before this congregation to be a loving, faithful and dutiful husband to her . . .' Not 'provided she is a loving, faithful and dutiful wife to you, do you promise . . .' That is not it at all. I say, 'Until death parts you from one another.' The covenant into which we enter is an unconditional covenant. It is not dependent on the response of the other party.

This is a wonderful thing. But it is only a shadow of the covenant God enters into with his people. This is why the LORD is described as 'the husband of his people' and Jesus is called our 'bridegroom'.

Yet we recognize that in human experience love does wither and even covenanted love fades. The response of the beloved changes love. Unfaithfulness can deal it a serious blow. But do you see what the eternal God says in verse 30–34?

If his sons forsake my law and do not follow my statutes, if they violate my decrees and fail to keep my commands, I will punish their sin with the rod . . . but *I will not take my love from him, nor will I ever betray my faithfulness.* I will not violate my covenant or alter what my lips have uttered.

The essence of God's covenant is that he enters into it unilaterally. Our love for him is a response, but not a conditioning factor.

God's love is so astonishing that we can scarcely grasp it. Because human love is affected by factors outside itself, we feel – quite wrongly – that God's love is also going to change. This is what the prodigal son thought when he went back to his father, saying, in effect, 'Things will certainly be changed now. There is no question about that. I can't imagine, after the mess I've made, that my father will accept me as a son again. I will say, "I am no more worthy to be called your son. Make me one of your hired servants." I will be glad to occupy that position, having forfeited all rights to the love I once knew.'

But when he made his little speech, his father said, 'I will do nothing of the kind. Bring the best robe. Kill the fatted calf.' He said that because his love for his son was unchanged.

That is a picture of God's covenanted, rock-like love for his people.

This does not mean that God is unmoved by our sin or careless about our rebellion – as we shall see. But it does mean that his love never alters. Though we are faithless, he remains faithful.

FAITHFUL IN HIS PROMISES

Third, God is faithful in his promises. That is included in the idea of the covenant. We see it in verses 3 and 4. There God swears that he will secure David's throne forever:

I have made a covenant with my chosen one,
I have sworn to David my servant,
'I will establish your line forever
and make your throne firm through all generations.'

Whenever God makes a covenant, he makes this kind of promise.

To Abraham, the promise was that his seed would be as the sand on the seashore. There were long years in which Abraham must have found the promise difficult to believe in. But the glorious thing is that God fulfilled his promise and that today we are able to read of the fulfilment.

We open the pages of our New Testament to Matthew 1:1, its very first verse, and what do we read? 'A record of the genealogy of Jesus Christ the son of David, the son of Abraham.' We see that God has fulfilled his promise and is continuing to work his sovereign purpose out.

God also puts signs in nature, as well as Scripture, to help us believe. When God covenanted with Noah, he put the sign of the rainbow in the sky. Do you remember what it meant? The rainbow was not to help God remember. It was not even to help us remember God's covenant. It was to help us remember that God remembers. That was the significance of it. It tells us that God will never betray his faithfulness or alter what his lips have uttered.

It is not only God's love which is allied to his faithfulness. God's power is also allied to it. It is his power which enables him to keep his promises. So the psalmist writes:

O LORD God Almighty, who is like you? You are mighty, O LORD, and your faithfulness surrounds you. You rule over the surging sea; when its waves mount up, you still them. You crushed Rahab like one of the slain; with your strong arm you scattered your enemies (*Psa.* 89:8–10).

What is the significance of this? Obviously, the psalmist is glorying in the might of God's strong arm, because it is God's power that enables him to keep the promises.

You know how we sometimes have difficulty keeping promises we have made. It is because we do not have the resources. We make financial promises, but we do not have sufficient financial resources to keep them. Or we may say to our children, 'I wish I could give this to you, but I can't. I do not have the money for it.' The psalmist is telling us that God is never embarrassed in this way. He has *all* power. He is the Lord Almighty. That is why God's words have to be taken with utmost seriousness.

We find this difficult because of our human background. When people make a promise to us, we often say, 'Do you really mean that?' We do this especially if the promise is surprising. We expect that people probably have not weighed what they are promising. By contrast, God's promises can be taken with absolute seriousness, because he has weighed them and there is nothing in them that he is not able to perform.

This is as true of God's threats as of his promises. Children soon get to know if parents issue threats they do not mean to keep. Scenes like one I witnessed on a transatlantic flight are commonplace. There was a family with three fairly small children who were particularly obstreperous. They were causing the cabin staff and people around them a great deal of trouble. Their father was raising his voice to them, saying, 'If you do that again, I'll do so and so.' One of the children looked around and smiled a little at those on the other side of the aisle, as if indicating that he knew his father would never fulfil what he was promising.

But when God warns us of the danger of some action, he means every word he says. The living, faithful God has never in all eternity uttered an idle word, and what he says, he will perform.

FAITHFUL IN HIS DISCIPLINE

Finally, notice that God is not only faithful in his nature, love and promises. He is faithful in his discipline:

If his sons forsake my law and do not follow my statutes, if they violate my decrees and fail to keep my commands, I will punish their sin with the rod, their iniquity with flogging (verses 30–32).

True love does not deny faithfulness in its discipline and correction; it expresses it there. It is the 'true son' whom the father chastises (*Heb.* 12:7, 8). God brings his children under discipline precisely because he loves them.

God's disciplining of our lives does not mean that he is forsaking his covenant. It means that he is exercising his covenant love in order to bring the blessings of his covenant to us. Therefore, he will not refrain from exercising discipline on us, bringing us under the weight of his hand in order that we might ultimately enter into the benefits of his covenant. That means that God's disciplines – whatever they may be in our lives – are never arbitrary or pointless. They are part of the faithful administration of his covenant.

God is faithful even when we are faithless, but not in the sense of being indifferent to our sins. He is faithful in his discipline.

God's faithfulness is designed to be both an encouragement and a challenge to us. There will be times in our lives when the reality of God's faithfulness will be clouded for us, as it was for the psalmist. Our faith will be tried, and we will be baffled by circumstances. Cherished plans will have been thwarted. Friends will have failed us, and Satan will have oppressed us. When this happens it is easy to conclude that God has revoked his covenant, forgotten his promises and abandoned his faithfulness. But when we are tempted to say that, we need to feed our souls on the truths of verses 33 and 34. God says:

I will not take my love from him, nor will I ever betray my faithfulness. I will not violate my covenant or alter what my lips have uttered.

Rest on that. That is the hope of our continuance in grace. It is the hope of our security, the foundation of our persevering in the Christian life – that God will remain faithful. We need to sing that truth in midwinter, like the psalmist.

But this truth is not only an encouragement. It is a challenge too. Theologians call faithfulness one of God's 'communicable attributes', distinguishing between those that are communicable and those that are incommunicable. There are some things, like God's omnipotence, that God does not share with us. None of us ever becomes like God in that sense.

But there are other aspects of God's character which, because they are part of his sanctifying purpose, he imparts to us by the Holy Spirit. Faithfulness is one of these. So we find Jesus saying, 'Be faithful, even to the point of death, and I will give you the crown of life' (*Rev.* 2:10). It is a characteristic of the good steward in Jesus' story: 'Well done, good and faithful servant' (Matt. 25:21 and 23).

God means to reproduce this consistency in us. To bring it right down into the marketplace, he means us to be men and women of our word. We are to be people of absolute integrity, whose 'yes' is 'yes' and whose 'no' is 'no'. People are to be able to trust us.

I know a man who serves in a senior position in an international bank. Somebody said to me about him, 'He is a man of Christian calibre and standing, of utter integrity.' Someone who had no Christian commitment of any kind said of him, 'The thing that stands out about that man is that he is straight down the line. He never wavers. You can trust everything he says.' I can think of no greater testimony to Christian character than that.

God knows that in our unfaithful world, where people are burned by disloyalty, denial of the truth and carelessness about facts, Christians need desperately to manifest the glory of God where he has put them so that people may become aware of God's faithfulness. They are to see it in our nature, our love and our promises – right through our character.

May God thus sanctify us that we may become like him.

5

THE GRACE OF GOD

*I*N HIS EXCELLENT BOOK, *Knowing God*, Dr J. I. Packer has
written these words: 'The grace of God is love freely shown
towards guilty sinners, contrary to their merit, and indeed in
defiance of their demerit. It is God showing goodness to persons
who deserve only severity, and had no reason to expect anything
but severity.'[1] God's grace is the keynote of Biblical Christianity,
and any attempt to understand the character of God must focus
upon the truth that God is 'the God of all grace' (*1 Pet.* 5:10), and
that the Christian message is 'the gospel of the grace of God' (*Acts*
20:24).

To help us think biblically about the nature of God's grace, we
must obviously turn to the Scriptures. The difficulty is that we have
an embarrassment of wealth in the material available to us. The
Bible overflows with this truth, but most recently God has been
speaking to me about his grace in one of the great verses of the
eighth chapter of Romans – verse 32 – and it is to that verse that
the rest of this chapter will be devoted.

Paul is writing to Christians at Rome who have been going
through the mill spiritually, suffering all kinds of trial and hard-
ship. His encouragement takes the form of a revelation of who
God is and what he is like, leading to the great challenge of
Romans 8:31, 'If God is for us, who can be against us?' Thereafter
he argues that the grace of God, revealed in the gospel, will be

[1] Downers Grove, Ill.: IVP, 1973, p. 120.

more than adequate for the needs of his children, whatever these may be. The very next verse (verse 32) takes us to the heart of how God has acted in sending his Son, which, if we grasp what is involved in this truth, will give us a cast-iron guarantee that in his infinite grace he will give us every lesser thing: 'He who did not spare his own Son, but gave him up for us all – how will he not also, along with him, graciously give us all things?' These words are packed full of truth, and we need to try to unpack it, even if only a little of it.

The verse has three parts to it. Part 1 tells us that 'God did not spare his own Son'; Part 2 tells us that 'He gave him up for us all'; and Part 3 is the conclusion Paul draws, 'How will he not also, along with him, graciously give us all things?' We ought to be able to dig deep into the truth of God's grace from these words.

1. 'GOD DID NOT SPARE HIS OWN SON.'

We are all familiar with the language of 'sparing' someone what is painful and causes suffering. Indeed, if we are parents, at a human level, and our children are going through some physical or mental anguish, or emotional suffering, we will naturally say, 'If it were in my power, I would gladly spare you this!'

Now God himself refers to that human emotion of a parent towards his child, and acknowledges that he experiences it at an infinite level:

> 'They will be mine,' says the LORD Almighty, 'in the day when I make up my treasured possession. I will spare them, just as in compassion a man spares his son who serves him' (*Mal.* 3:17).

Yet, here is the great mystery. God did not spare his own Son. Notice how that Son is described: he is God's own, or only, or only begotten Son. The point is that God has many sons and daughters by adoption, but the Lord Jesus Christ is his only begotten son.

58

You remember how he was described at the moment when heaven opened at the descent of the Spirit of God upon him: 'This is my Son, whom I love; with him I am well pleased' (*Matt.* 4:17). But God the Father did not spare that beloved Son.

Of course, the classic occasion in the whole of the Old Testament when a man did not spare his own son occurs in the account of Abraham ascending Mount Moriah, with Isaac, his one and only son. God had commanded him to take Isaac and sacrifice him: 'Take your son, your only son, Isaac, whom you love, and go to the region of Moriah. Sacrifice him there' (*Gen.* 22:2). So Abraham saddled his donkey and took two servants and his son, Isaac, and set off for Moriah. When they arrived there, Abraham built an altar, bound his son Isaac, laid him on the altar, and took the knife to slay him.

But the angel of the LORD called out to him from heaven, 'Do not lay a hand on the boy.' And Abraham looked up and saw a ram caught by its horns in a thicket and recognized it as the provision of God's grace. So he sacrificed it as a burnt offering, instead of his son. Genesis 22:16 records what God said to him at that point: 'Because you have done this, and have not withheld your son, your only son, I will surely bless you.'

You see what has happened? Even though Abraham did not spare him, God did – he intervened and provided a substitute for Isaac, to die in his place. But the great mystery lies precisely here: for God's own Son, there was no substitute. God did not spare him. And this is the more remarkable when you think that Jesus cried out in Gethsemane to be spared: 'My Father, if it is possible, may this cup be taken from me.' But God the Father did not spare his own Son.

Now, inevitably, we ask the question, 'Why was this? Why did Jesus' plea go unanswered? Was it because the Father's love for the Son had changed?'

All heaven would respond, 'Never.' But the question remains; and the answer is found in this way: when we see Abraham not sparing Isaac, we cry out, 'How he loved God!' And when we see God not sparing Christ, we need to cry out, 'How God loved me!' He did not spare his own Son, but gave him up for us all. It is this truth which causes the hymn writers to be overwhelmed and cry, 'Amazing love', 'Love so amazing, so divine', 'Amazing grace', 'Love divine, all loves excelling', 'O Christ, what love is this?'

This is God the Father and God the Son united in a love for sinners that must make the universe tremble. And it is this that ultimately persuades Paul that God is a God of grace, of undeserved, unmerited love. The reason there could be no substitute for God's Son was that he was the Substitute for sinners:

> In my place condemned He stood,
> Sealed my pardon with His blood.

That is the ultimate evidence of the grace of God.

2. 'HE GAVE HIM UP FOR US ALL.'

That is, in a sense, the positive side of what Paul is saying: 'He did not spare his own Son, but gave him up [or delivered him up] for us all.'

Significantly, that is a phrase you find recurring again and again in the Gospel accounts of Jesus' suffering and death. It is used of Judas giving up Jesus to the Jews: 'What are you willing to give me if I hand him over [it is the same word] to you?' (*Matt.* 26:15). It is said of the Jews handing over Jesus to the Gentiles in Matthew 20:18–19: 'They will condemn him to death and will turn him over [the same word] to the Gentiles to be mocked and flogged and crucified.' It is used of the Jews handing Jesus over to Pilate in Matthew 27:1–2: 'They bound him, led him away, and turned him over [the same word] to Pilate.' But here in Romans 8:32,

Paul says, 'It was God the Father who gave him up, delivered him over.' In the nineteenth century, Octavius Winslow wrote these memorable words: 'Who delivered up Jesus to die? Not Judas, for money; not Pilate, for fear; not the Jews, for envy;—but the Father, for love!'[1] That is what God the Father was doing at Calvary, and it is the ultimate expression of his free, unmerited grace.

We will only grasp this truth if we recollect what the Father was giving up, or handing over, the Son to suffer. The Bible unfolds this to us in terms of what Christ *became*. In Philippians 2:7–8, Paul tells us that he who was in very nature God and shared the Father's glory became *man*, with all that that involved. But not only did he become man, he became a *servant*: he whom angels and archangels had been created to serve became himself a servant; but that was only the beginning. In 2 Corinthians 5:21 Paul tells us that Jesus became *sin* for us. He who knew no sin actually became sin to accomplish our salvation. Then in Galatians 3:13 the apostle takes us into depths we simply cannot fathom when he tells us that the Son of God, in whom the Father was well pleased, 'became a *curse*' for us. The grace of God to sinners is exhibited in the cry of Jesus on Calvary, 'My God, my God, why have you forsaken me?'

You will notice the three words which follow 'gave him up' in our text. They are the words, 'for us all'. That use of the word 'all' means, not 'all without exception', but 'all without distinction' – the implication being that there is no sinner too bad, no life too marred, no heart too hardened, no soul who has drifted too far, for the grace of God to bring that soul to himself in Jesus Christ and to make him a new creature. I am told there was an old Scottish preacher who used to speak often of 'the long arm of grace'.[2]

---

[1] *No Condemnation in Christ Jesus* (1853; repr. Edinburgh: Banner of Truth), p. 361.

[2] Similarly, John Newton says, 'Grace has long and strong arms' (*Wise Counsel: John Newton's Letters to John Ryland, Jr.*, Edinburgh: Banner of Truth, 2009, p. 364).

3. 'HOW WILL HE NOT ALSO, ALONG WITH HIM, GRACIOUSLY GIVE US ALL THINGS?'

The apostle's conclusion depends on the fact that we have the evidence before us that all God's dealings are gracious. Professor John Murray points out that the interrogatory form confronts us with 'the unthinkableness of the opposite'![1]

The contrasts are striking. The grace of God is measured by the fact that he has given and not withheld his own Son. How then could we suspect that he might withhold any lesser thing from us? Whatever we need throughout our Christian pilgrimage, we have a guarantee in God's incomparable grace that he will supply it.

That includes strength for the weak, hope for the despairing, peace for the restless; supplies for needs that we could never have foreseen, and circumstances that we could never have envisaged. Nothing is excluded from this divine guarantee, since the grace of God is without measure.

Notice that all that God provides for us in his grace is 'along with him'. We need to remember that God's grace does not simply mean that Christ was given for us. It also means that by that grace all things along with Christ are given to us. All the riches of God are in Christ Jesus, and these riches are 'unsearchable' (*Eph.* 3:8).

What conclusions, then, do we need to draw from this teaching for our own lives? Perhaps some who read these pages are troubled about sin and failure in the past, and are cast down because it seems that nothing could be adequate to deal with their guilt and shame. I must tell you that the grace of God is always greater than your greatest sin. Paul puts it strikingly in Romans 5:20 (KJV): 'Where sin abounded, grace did much more abound.' Perhaps others are apprehensive about the future. Knowing your own past weakness and tendency to stray, you fear the unknown

[1] *Romans*, vol. 1, *New London Commentary on the New Testament* (London: Marshall, Morgan and Scott, 1960), p. 326

future, and the threatening complexities of the twenty-first century. You need to know that the God of all grace is not the great 'I was', but the great 'I AM', whose 'love is as great as his power, and knows neither measure nor end' (to use the words of Joseph Hart's hymn).[1]

So, hold back from God no longer. Let his matchless grace embrace you. Trust him utterly for every area of your life. Put your confidence in him alone. After all, where could it more safely lie?

> Sovereign grace o'er sin abounding,
> Ransomed souls, the tidings swell;
> 'Tis a deep that knows no sounding
> Who its breadth or length can tell?
> On its glories
> Let my soul for ever dwell.
>
> JOHN KENT 1766–1843

[1] 'How good is the God we adore', by Joseph Hart, 1712–68.

PART TWO

THE SALVATION OF GOD

6

REGENERATION: BEGINNING WITH GOD

I SPENT THE FIRST FIFTEEN YEARS of my ministry in a small country town in Ayrshire in Scotland. Not far from there, in the seventeenth century, a godly man named David Dickson ministered in the town of Irvine. Some remarkable revivals broke out, associated with a series of sermons on the subject of regeneration. That often seems to have happened in times of revival. The history of revival bears witness to the frequency with which regeneration was a theme accompanying it. David Dickson preached twenty-seven sermons in his series, which is more like the time scale for the subject of regeneration, I would think, than one occasion. But in the midst of it he gave this definition:

> Regeneration is the work of God's invincible power and mere grace, wherein by his Spirit accompanying his Word he quickeneth a redeemed person lying dead in his sins and reneweth him in his mind, his will and all the powers of his soul, convincing him savingly of sin and righteousness and judgment, and making him heartily to embrace Christ and salvation, and to consecrate himself to the service of God in Christ all the days of his life.[1]

It would be difficult to find a more satisfying summary of regeneration than that.

[1] David Dickson, *Select Practical Writings*, vol. 1 (Edinburgh: The Free Church of Scotland, 1845), p. 211.

The place where we may best come to grips with this theme biblically is in the third chapter of John's Gospel. Here our Lord is presenting this truth to Nicodemus, a ruler of the Jews and a teacher in Israel. Not that the teaching of Jesus in John 3 is unique or out of harmony with the rest of his teaching in the Gospels! Indeed, the doctrine of regeneration which is taught in this chapter is really the logical link – as John Murray points out[1] – between our Lord's teaching on the pollution and depravity of the natural human heart, on the one hand, and the demands and requirements of membership of his kingdom, on the other. There is a tremendous gulf between the teaching of our Lord on the depravity and sickness of the human heart, including the inability of man by nature, and the requirements which he urges upon us as members of his kingdom. The logical and vital link between these two is regeneration. We can summarize our Lord's teaching in this passage under several headings: the *necessity* of regeneration, the *nature* of regeneration, the *origin* of regeneration, the *manner* of regeneration, the *marks* of regeneration and the *context* within which regeneration occurs.

THE NECESSITY OF REGENERATION: YOU MUST BE BORN AGAIN

The necessity of regeneration could scarcely be put more categorically than in Jesus' words in John 3, verses 3, 5 and 7: 'I tell you the truth, unless a man is born again, he cannot see the kingdom of God . . . I tell you the truth, unless a man is born of water and the Spirit, he cannot enter the kingdom of God . . . You should not be surprised at my saying, "You must be born again."' This necessity has certain specific characteristics.

First, it is an *indispensable* necessity. I mean by that, that there are some things more important than others, even amongst the things

---

[1] *Redemption Accomplished and Applied* (1955, 1961; repr. Edinburgh: Banner of Truth, 2009), Part 2, chapter 3: *Regeneration*, p. 91.

which Scripture presses upon us, and that regeneration is among those items of utmost importance. That is the significance of our Lord's words in verses 3 and 5 – 'I tell you the truth [literally, truly, truly].' They are a kind of underlining. Here Jesus is underlining his words to emphasize their significance for us. There are some things that a man may dispense with and still enter the kingdom of God. He may enter the kingdom of God without ever being baptized or sitting at the Lord's Table. These are important. But they are not indispensable. By contrast, what Jesus is here describing is an indispensable necessity, for a man will never in all eternity enter the kingdom of God without being regenerated by the Holy Spirit.

Second, it is a *universal* necessity. Not everything Jesus says is a universal necessity. For example, he said to the rich young ruler that he must sell all that he had and give to the poor. But Jesus does not tell everybody to sell all that he or she has and give to the poor. That was necessary for him but not for everybody. However, Jesus' words about regeneration are of a different order. Jesus said, 'Unless a man is born again,' and this means that regeneration was a necessity for Nicodemus personally precisely because regeneration is a necessity for all men universally.

The universal nature of this necessity derives from the fact that by nature every human being is defiled, deadened and corrupted by sin. This is what Jesus is referring to when he says: 'Flesh gives birth to flesh, but the Spirit gives birth to spirit' (*John* 3:6). 'Flesh' here means human nature as it is dominated and polluted by sin. So what Jesus is telling us is that unrenewed human nature dominated by sin can only reproduce itself.

Regeneration is a universal necessity because man (using the term generically to mean every man and woman) by his own fleshly effort has a universal inability to produce anything except the flesh. No amount of education will produce regeneration. No amount of external religion will do anything to change this basic position. This is the law of generation, which you find illustrated in the first part of Genesis: 'Creatures . . . according to their kinds' (*Gen.* 1:21). Man brings forth flesh from his flesh, and sinful flesh remains sinful flesh. So Jesus says, 'You should not be surprised at my saying, "You must be born again"' (*John* 3:7). The new birth is a universal necessity because the disabling, defiling power of sin is universal.

But Nicodemus misunderstands all this. He thinks that Jesus is speaking about a new physical start. If only a man could be born again in the sense of entering his mother's womb a second time! Nicodemus thinks that Jesus is referring to this kind of new beginning. But this would not help in the slightest, because a thousand new starts would only produce the same weary tale of defeat, pollution and disablement. It is a new nature, a new heart which man needs. That is, he needs to be born of the Spirit.

This is a very important thing for us to grasp, because the point is not merely academic. It is significant for our evangelism. We need to recognize that man is not just confused and in need of greater clarity in his thinking, nor does he merely need to be redirected into the ways of God, nor is it only the fact that he is guilty and needs to be forgiven. His problem is that he is dead and needs to be resurrected. He needs new life. Our evangelism needs to be based on this foundation. We need rightly to diagnose the problem of man before we ever begin rightly to understand the gospel that he needs. We may help a man to understand his confusion and lead him into the right way. We may indoctrinate him. But the one thing that we can never do is regenerate him, and this is why our Lord is at pains to lay down the universal necessity of regeneration.

But regeneration is not only an indispensable and universal necessity; it is also an *unchangeable* necessity.

It is unchangeable because of the issues with which it deals. Jesus' teaching in John 3:3–5 shows that regeneration deals not with passing, changing things but with the unchanging laws of God concerning his kingdom – how a man may perceive the kingdom and enter it:

> Jesus declared, 'I tell you the truth, unless a man is born again he cannot see the kingdom of God.'
> 'How can a man be born when he is old?' Nicodemus asked. 'Surely he cannot enter a second time into his mother's womb to be born!'
> Jesus answered, 'I tell you the truth, unless a man is born of water and the Spirit, he cannot enter the kingdom of God.'

The kingdom of God is the sphere in which God brings rebel sinners into subjection to his gracious rule and authority. It is the realm in which God's grace is to be tested and experienced. To 'see' the kingdom is to grasp or understand it, to have the glory and wonder of it dawn upon us. But this will never dawn upon a man until he has been born again. Similarly, to 'enter' the kingdom of God means to experience the blessings of the kingdom, to be admitted to its privileges and joys both present and future. But apart from the new birth, says Jesus, we shall never experience any of these joys. This is an unchanging necessity because it deals with these unchanging laws of God's kingdom.

THE NATURE OF REGENERATION: A NEW CREATION

What, then, is this work of grace which is an indispensable, universal and unchangeable necessity? It is a radical, total change in sinful man accomplished solely by God the Holy Spirit, producing new life – what Paul calls 'a new creation'. The very metaphor that our Lord uses in his conversation with Nicodemus leads into the nature of it, for he is saying that regeneration is as momentous as birth itself.

It is significant that the New Testament uses such radical language to describe Christian beginnings, language like resurrection, regeneration and re-creation. It teaches us that being brought out of darkness into light is something that can only be paralleled by creation, birth, or resurrection from the dead. It is like a new life beginning. It is parallel, if you like, to a new creation. 'God, who said, "Let light shine out of darkness", made his light shine in our hearts to give us the light of the knowledge of the glory of God in the face of Christ' (2 *Cor.* 4:6).

One of the things we need so much to grasp in our day is the wonder of what happened to us when we were born into the kingdom of God's grace. I am sure that one of the reasons people are looking for additional, secondary thrills offered at some future stage in their spiritual experience is that they have devalued the initial work of grace. We speak as though it were something we had done, something anyone can do. But the Bible describes it as the miracle of resurrection, as the miracle of a new creation.

This is something which we greatly misunderstand when we speak, as we often do, about people who have been saved from some particularly dissolute context in society and some particularly debauched kind of life. I remember a young boy who had been a gang leader in the district where I originally served as a pastor. He had committed just about every sin you could imagine, but he was saved by Christ and was brought into the church. People used to say to me, 'Well, you know, it really took a miracle to save him!' I was very interested when I heard that, because the implication was that it took something less than a miracle to save respectable sinners like us!

These people had not really understood the reality or nature of the total depravity of every man, whatever form it takes, or the resurrection that God performs when he raises anyone into new-ness of life in Christ.

This is what is involved in the well-known phrase 'born again', which occurs in verses 3 and 5. It is exactly what Henry Scougal called it, in the title of his famous little book (which had such an astonishing influence on men like George Whitefield), *The Life of God in the Soul of Man*. That title expresses exactly what regenera-tion is. As John himself said, it is having God's nature abiding in you because you are 'born of God' (*1 John* 3:9).

Regeneration is characterized by both cleansing and renewal. 'Jesus answered, "I tell you the truth, unless a man is born of water and the Spirit, he cannot enter the kingdom of God."'

Being born of water does not refer to baptism. That would be to interpret Jesus as reinforcing the Pharisees' false notion that inward spiritual problems can be resolved by external physical rites. We need to look rather at verse 10 for help in understanding verse 5: 'You are Israel's teacher,' said Jesus, 'and do you not understand these things?' Here Jesus is gently chiding Nicodemus for not understanding him, despite his night visitor being a teacher of Israel.

What was God's great promise to Israel to which Jesus refers? It was, surely, the words of Ezekiel 36:25, 26, where the prophet says on God's behalf, 'I will sprinkle clean water on you, and you will be clean.' This is the promise of the new age and of the Mes-siah's coming. 'I will give you a new heart and put a new spirit in you.' That is the double promise of spiritual cleansing and spiritual renewal.

Similarly, this is how Paul characterizes the regenerating work of the Holy Spirit:

At one time we too were foolish, disobedient, deceived and enslaved by all kinds of passions and pleasures. We lived in malice and envy, being hated and hating one another. But when the kindness and love of God our Saviour appeared, he saved us, not because of righteous things we had done, but because of his mercy. He saved us through the washing of rebirth and the renewal by the Holy Spirit (*Titus* 3:3–5)

Regeneration deals with two things, then: the pollution of our nature, and the perversity of our wills. God implants a spirit of obedience to give us a new heart, and he grants us cleansing to take away our defilement. The essence of the new birth is this supernatural work of grace effected by the Holy Spirit – a work akin to a new creation of new life. And it has this double character of cleansing and renewal.

THE ORIGIN OF REGENERATION: BORN FROM ABOVE

Who is the author of the new birth and to whom do we look for it? This question leads us to the source of the new birth and to our Lord's clear teaching that the author of the new birth is God the Holy Spirit:

> Unless a man is born of water and the Spirit . . . The Spirit gives birth to spirit . . . The wind blows wherever it pleases. You hear its sound, but you cannot tell where it comes from or where it is going. So it is with everyone born of the Spirit (*John* 3:5,6,8)

As someone has put it, the Holy Spirit is the womb out of which the new birth comes. Jesus emphasizes the same truth in another way when he speaks of being born 'from above' (verse 3). Most of the translations say either 'born again' or 'born anew'. But Jesus really says, 'Unless one is born from above.' The Greek word is *anōthen*.

William Still of Aberdeen, who was instrumental in the growth of a work of grace among evangelical ministers in Scotland during the second half of the twentieth century, once had a large and striking poster put outside his church. Providentially the buses stopped, sometimes for a protracted time, outside his church on Union Street in Aberdeen. So he had this large board erected on the church wall which one day bore this message: 'You must be born *anōthen.*' Many people stopped and stared at this. The morning it went up he had a telephone call from a business house in Aberdeen, and the man on the line said to him, 'Sir, I was passing your church this morning and saw this ridiculous notice you have up. What does it mean? You must be born *anōthen.*'

'Oh,' William Still said, 'it means you must be born from above. It means that from below, that is, from man, there is no hope of eternal life. It must come from above, from God.'

His caller chided, 'Well, why couldn't you simply have put *that* up in your notice?'

He answered, 'Then people like you would never phone me up and give me the opportunity of telling you what I have just said!'

The word *anōthen* is the same word that is used in the conversation between Jesus and Pilate in John 19:11 ('You would have no power over me if it were not given to you *from above')* and again in John 3:31 ('The one who comes *from above* is above all'), where Jesus is contrasting coming from the earth, that is, from man, and coming from God. The implication is clear. The new birth has its source in God alone. The metaphor itself underlines the point. Jesus is saying that a man can no more procure his own spiritual birth than he was able to undertake his own physical conception and procreation. So the one thing that is necessary for us is the one thing we cannot do for ourselves.

Now some might say: 'But that would drive us to despair, if we believed that. How are we to preach this to men?' But that is precisely the point. It is the effect we want. Says C. H. Spurgeon:

> 'Ah!' says somebody, 'I fear that this kind of preaching will
> be very discouraging to a great many people.' Well, how will
> it discourage them? 'It will discourage them from trying to

save themselves.' That is the very thing that I want to do. I would like not only to discourage them from attempting that impossible task, but to cast them into despair concerning it. When a man utterly despairs of being able to save himself, it is then that he cries to God to save him, so I believe that we cannot do a man a better turn than to discourage him from ever resting upon anything that he can do towards saving himself.[1]

This is not an academic question. It affects me if I am *not* born anew. To whom do I look for the new birth? To whom shall I apply for it? It affects me if I *am* born anew. To whom shall I give all the glory, honour and praise for the new birth? It affects me if there are *other people* whose new birth I desire. To whom shall I look for their regeneration? What is the work that is going to be significant in producing regeneration? The proper answer to those questions will make us realize that prayer is fundamental and not supplemental in the work of evangelism.

The theological terms to which this question points particularly are *monergism* and *synergism*. Monergism means '*one person* [as in monotheistic, one God] *working* [as in *energy*]'. Synergism means '*persons working together*'. Our Lord is saying that regeneration belongs to the realm of monergism. Only God is at work in regeneration. Do we contribute anything? Oh yes, we do! The one thing that you and I contribute to our salvation is the sin which makes it necessary.

THE MANNER OF REGENERATION: WHERE AND WHEN GOD WILLS

Jesus also teaches us here about the *manner* of the new birth. He draws a comparison between the activity of the wind and the

---

[1] *Metropolitan Tabernacle Pulpit,* LIV (1908), pp. 585–6.

activity of the Spirit: 'The wind blows wherever it pleases. You hear its sound, but you cannot tell where it comes from or where it is going. So it is with everyone born of the Spirit' (*John* 3:8).

The word for 'wind' and the word for 'spirit' are one and the same in Greek, the language in which the Gospel is written. Our Lord seems to be making a comparison. He is saying that the manner of the Spirit's work in regeneration is like the operation of the wind. That is marked by several things.

First, it is marked by *efficacy*. The wind blows; it has a dynamic within it. There is an effect when the wind is blowing. In many parts of the world the wind has a tremendous efficacy. When it blows things bend before it that nothing else will bend. Jesus is saying that wherever the Spirit of God is blowing he leaves new creations in his wake. There is an efficacy in the Spirit's power as he moves in regenerating grace.

There is also a *sovereignty* to the Spirit's work, for the wind blows 'where it wills.' I remember being given the opportunity to sail on the Firth of Clyde, a beautiful part of Scotland, where on some days we were becalmed and used to wish that we could command the wind to come. But the wind cannot be commanded like that. Or, on the other hand, some days there may be wild storms and you might wish to command the wind to stop. But the wind has a sovereignty of its own; it blows where it wills. And so does the Holy Spirit, who is sovereign in his work of regeneration.

That is why we are often completely surprised by the way God is working and why we must not try to drag the sovereign work of the Holy Spirit down to the level of our own manipulation. If you had taken a poll in the churches of Judea in the period around the death of Stephen (recorded in Acts 8), asking who was the least likely man to be converted, Saul of Tarsus would have come pretty close to the top of the poll. But in his sovereignty the Holy Spirit moved where he would and regenerated Paul.

There is also a *mystery* about the wind. You cannot tell, says Jesus, where it comes from or where it is going. We must never seek to remove either this element of sovereignty or this element of mystery from the Spirit's work.

God by his Holy Spirit often comes in mysterious ways to bring people to new birth.

THE MARKS OF REGENERATION

C. R. Vaughan speaks of the reality of regeneration as an inference to be drawn from evidence. He urges in his book *The Gifts of the Holy Spirit* (which I commend), that the inference be drawn cautiously and deliberately, not hurriedly.[1]

We can see some of the evidence for which we look in our Lord's own words to Nicodemus: 'Flesh gives birth to flesh, but the Spirit gives birth to spirit' (verse 6). That is, there are works of the flesh (which Paul elaborates in Galatians 5:19-21) by which the flesh is recognized. And there are works of the Spirit (which Paul elaborates in Galatians 5:22, 23) by which the Spirit is recognized.

All spiritual activities depend on God's Spirit. J. I. Packer has put it with typical conciseness in this way: '*There are no spiritual activities without regeneration*.'[2] But here is the other side to it: 'There is no regeneration without spiritual activities.' No spiritual activities without regeneration and no regeneration without spiritual activities. The sign of the Spirit blowing, that is, the recognizable signs of his presence, is the fruit of the Spirit. John himself spells out some of these marks in his first epistle.

In 1 John 2:29, he teaches that *the practice of righteousness* is one evidence of regeneration: 'If you know that he is righteous, you

[1] C. R. Vaughan, *The Gifts of the Holy Spirit* (1894 edition, reprinted Edinburgh: Banner of Truth, 1975), pp. 191–207.

[2] J. I. Packer, *God's Words* (Leicester: Inter-Varsity Press, 1981) p. 151. Italics in original.

know that everyone who does what is right has been born of him.' Another mark is *a departure from the practice of sinning,* as in 1 John 3:9: 'No one who is born of God will continue to sin,' that is, the way he did before. 1 John 4:7 speaks of *the practice of love:* 'Dear friends, let us love one another, for love comes from God. Everyone who loves has been born of God and knows God.' We also find *the exercise of faith* in 1 John 5:1: 'Everyone who believes that Jesus is the Christ is born of God.' So faith, too, is an evidence of regeneration. And then 1 John 5:4 stresses that *the victory over the world* is an evidence of regeneration: 'Everyone born of God has overcome the world.'

This, too, is not mere theology. It is precisely what we see happening when true regeneration takes place.

During my ministry in St George's-Tron Church in Glasgow the Royal Academy of Music was located beside our building. At one time God began to do some remarkable things through the Christian Union in the Academy. I would regularly get telephone calls asking, 'Could you see so and so? Could you go and see someone?'

One of the students called me once and said, 'I've made an appointment for somebody to see you.' (It's one of the lovely things students do. They imagine that you don't have anything else scheduled!) She said, 'I've made an appointment for you to see so-and-so today at two. I think he wants to become a Christian, and we're trying to help him.'

I met this young man at two, and we got to know each other a little. Then I said to him, 'Now, tell me about what's been happening to you.'

He said, 'Well, that's what I want to know. I don't know what's been happening to me. But I've suddenly discovered that I'm longing to read the Bible. I've found that Jesus has become everything in life to me! I want to know God! The things I longed to do before have begun to die away, and things I never thought I would be longing after, these are beginning to be the great things in my life!'

I said, 'But somebody said to me that you wanted to *become* a Christian! You already are!' For these were precisely the evidences of regeneration in the boy's heart. God had given him newness of life in Christ.

THE CONTEXT IN WHICH REGENERATION OCCURS: THE WORD OF TRUTH

John's Gospel presents the truth of rebirth which Jesus taught Nicodemus in the context of the preaching of a crucified Saviour:

> I tell you the truth, we speak of what we know, and we testify to what we have seen, but still you people do not accept our testimony. I have spoken to you of earthly things and you do not believe; how then will you believe if I speak of heavenly things? No one has ever gone into heaven except the one who came from heaven – the Son of Man. Just as Moses lifted up the snake in the desert, so the Son of Man must be lifted up, that everyone who believes in him may have eternal life (*John* 3:11–16).

The context of regeneration in our Lord's conversation with Nicodemus is the preaching of the gospel. Indeed, the sovereign Spirit employs the instrumentality of the Word in the production of regeneration. As Peter reminds us in 1 Peter 1:23, 'For you have been born again, not of perishable seed, but of imperishable, through the living and enduring word of God.' Similarly, in James 1:18: 'He chose to give us birth through the word of truth.' This means that the context in which God creates newness of life is the reading and the preaching of, and testimony to, the Word of God, whether publicly or privately. The Word of God is the instrument the Holy Spirit is pleased to use.

Professor John Murray says, 'Regenerative grace is carried to us in the bosom of the effectual call, and since the latter is by the Word we must never think of regeneration . . . as wrought outside of a context that has reality and meaning only as a result of the Word.'[1]

That is why, in his great work on this theme, the Puritan Stephen Charnock urges us to prize the Word of God as the Spirit's mighty instrument in regeneration. He says it is an instrument to unlock the prison doors, and take them off the hinges, to strike off the fetters, and draw out the soul into a glorious liberty. Nothing else ever wrought such miraculous change. Therefore:

> Prize the word of truth, which works such great effects in the soul. Value that as long as you live, which is the cord where-by God hath drawn any of you out of the dungeon of death . . . If a soul be worth a world, and therefore to be prized, how precious ought that to be which is an instrument to beget a soul for the felicity of another world! How should the law of God's mouth be better to us than thousands of gold and silver! Psalm 119:72. How should we prize that word whereby any of us have seen the glory of God in his sanctuary, the glory of God in our souls! When corruptions are strong, it is an engine to batter them; when our hearts are hard, it is a hammer to break them; . . . when our hearts are cold, it is a fire to enflame them; when our souls are faint, it is a cordial to refresh them, it begins a new birth and maintains it . . . Have a great regard to it, keep it in the midst of your hearts, for it is life, Prov. 4:21, 22.[2]

---

[1] John Murray, *Collected Writings*, vol. 2, *Select Lectures* in *Systematic Theology* (Edinburgh: Banner of Truth, 1977), pp. 197–8.
[2] Stephen Charnock, *The Complete Works*, vol. 3 (Edinburgh: James Nichol, 1865), pp. 326-7. Reprinted Edinburgh: Banner of Truth, 1984.

That is why we are concerned with a ministry, life, and evangelism that are utterly biblical, not only conforming to biblical truth but with biblical content. Our confidence must be in the Word of God in its saving power, under the ministry of God's Holy Spirit.

What should this doctrine of regeneration do for us, then? There are at least four things:

It should thrill our souls with a new sense of worship as we observe the sheer miracle that God has performed in us in this regenerating grace.

It should enlarge our understanding of what it means to be redeemed.

It should drive us to God in a new way for those who are yet without eternal life, recognizing that it is he and he alone who can bring that life to men and women.

It should bow us down before him in wonder that the God of all the ages, the Creator of the universe, should apply such mighty works of power to the souls of men and women, in order to raise us into new life, and to conform us to the beautiful image of his Son.

7

JUSTIFICATION: THE GLORIOUS GOOD NEWS OF GRACE

N O ONE TRULY UNDERSTANDS the heart of the Christian message who does not understand justification. Martin Luther once said, 'It is this which makes true Christians; if justification is lost, all true Christianity is lost.'

In Galatians 2:15–21, Paul introduces us to this word which is so central to the message of Christianity – indeed central to everything that makes Christianity distinctive.

> We who are Jews by birth and not 'Gentile sinners' know that a man is not justified by observing the law, but by faith in Jesus Christ. So we, too, have put our faith in Christ Jesus that we may be justified by faith in Christ and not by observing the law, because by observing the law no-one will be justified.

> If, while we seek to be justified in Christ, it becomes evident that we ourselves are sinners, does that mean that Christ promotes sin? Absolutely not! If I rebuild what I destroyed, I prove that I am a law-breaker. For through the law I died to the law, so that I might live for God. I have been crucified with Christ, and I no longer live, but Christ lives in me. The life I live in the body, I live by faith in the Son of God, who loved me and gave himself for me. I do not set aside the grace of God, for if righteousness could be gained through the law, Christ died for nothing.

To understand what Paul is telling us here, we must ask three questions: *First*, what does justification mean? *Second*, how can it happen? *Third*, what is its result?

WHAT IS JUSTIFICATION?

We borrow the legal term justification from the world of the law courts. To *justify* someone is to pronounce him not guilty, innocent, righteous in the presence of the judge.

Its exact opposite is condemnation; to *condemn* someone is to declare him guilty.

Picture, if you will, a man brought into the presence of God, who is both his Creator and his Judge. The man waits for the verdict to be pronounced upon him by the Judge of all the earth, knowing that the verdict will determine his final destiny. Justification is such a verdict, and the whole of biblical teaching on the subject links the present-day verdict which God passes upon us now with the verdict that he will pass upon us on that last day.

In the Bible, justification is more than a pardon, acquittal, or forgiveness. It is all of these, but much more. It means that God as our Judge actually accepts us as righteous, just as he accepts his only begotten Son as righteous. And when God pronounces the verdict 'justified' over us, he is accepting us into his presence as completely righteous, for all eternity.

The amazing transition which biblical justification represents is like that of a criminal, awaiting a terrible sentence, being told instead that he is in fact heir to a fabulous inheritance. It is a verdict not only given by God, but which, once given, is irrevocable. It is the verdict of that last day, the day of final judgment, brought into the present so that the apostle Paul may say in Romans 8:1, 'Therefore, there is now no condemnation for those who are in Christ Jesus.' That is, condemnation is something with which we are finished forever, if we are justified by God.

HOW CAN JUSTIFICATION OCCUR?

How can God, who is the judge of all the earth, take guilty sinners like ourselves and accept us as innocent and righteous, welcoming us as he welcomes his only begotten Son?

This question is critical.

In Exodus 23:7, God quite specifically says, 'I will not justify the wicked' (KJV). In Deuteronomy 25:1–3 he instructs the judges in Israel that they must justify the righteous and condemn the wicked. Yet Paul actually speaks of God as the God who justifies the ungodly (*Rom.* 4:5, KJV).

How can that happen? In Galatians 2:16, Paul raises two possible answers: either I can earn it, or someone else can earn it for me. Justification could come by observing the law, or it could come by faith in Christ.

Now, the *first* of these two options is certainly what the Jewish teachers espoused. Misunderstanding the Old Testament, they believed that if you wanted to be justified, accepted, acquitted of your sin, and welcomed into the presence of God, then the only possible answer was sheer hard work – observing and keeping the Law of God, principally the Ten Commandments.

There is only one thing wrong with that solution. No one can do it; nor has anyone ever done it, with the singular exception of Jesus. Paul himself says 'If I rebuild what I destroyed, then I prove that I am a lawbreaker' (*Gal.* 2:18). That is our nature, our tendency; everything within us turns us toward breaking the law rather than keeping it. That is the problem with a religion which says to people, 'Now all you have to do is keep the Ten Commandments and live by the Sermon on the Mount, and everything will be wonderful.' Any honest man or woman who attempts this will admit, 'Out of the ashes of my failure, I must tell you that I do not need a lecture to tell me how to live, I need a Saviour to prevent me from living the way I naturally do.'

The *second* answer is that I may be justified by faith in Jesus Christ as the One who lived a perfect, sinless life in obedience to the law and died on the cross in my place, bearing my judgment as he suffered God's punishment against sin.

Many will say, 'I don't really understand why God needs Jesus Christ to die as a substitute to bear the judgment of my sins. I forgive other people out of the generosity of my heart, saying, "You are forgiven; I'm sorry you did it. I hope you will not do it again."'

The mistake they make, however, is believing that God – like us – is a mere private individual. He is not. He is the Judge of the whole earth; and when we appear before him, we stand before him in that capacity. You see, therefore, that it is impossible for God merely to forgive our sin and acquit us of it simply because he loves us. God does not act as a private individual, as it were, but as the One who upholds truth and righteousness and justice, because he is a God of infinite holiness, justice, and truth.

What, then, did God do? Paul tells us that he set forth his only begotten Son so that the judgment and punishment of all our sin might rest upon him who, for our sake, has been perfectly obedient to the Father. He bore the judgment that comes from the throne of God. And the deeper mystery is that this Lord Jesus Christ, who loved me and gave himself for me, is himself God. In his incarnation and his obedience to death, he has stepped down from the throne of judgment to the place of judgment, taken our place, and borne the judgment of our sin. Therefore, sinners are justified by the free gift of God's grace in Jesus Christ.

WHAT IS THE RESULT OF JUSTIFICATION?

In Galatians 2:17–21, Paul deals with a common objection to the doctrine of justification by faith in Jesus Christ alone.

If, while we seek to be justified in Christ, it becomes evident that we ourselves are sinners, does that mean that Christ promotes sin? Absolutely not! If I rebuild what I destroyed, I prove that I am a lawbreaker. For through the law I died to the law so that I might live for God. I have been crucified with Christ and I no longer live, but Christ lives in me. The life I live in the body, I live by faith in the Son of God, who loved me and gave himself for me. I do not set aside the grace of God, for if righteousness could be gained through the law, Christ died for nothing!

There were those who suggested that this teaching caused people to be morally careless and even encouraged them to sin so that they might be forgiven more.

Paul says that if this is how you regard the results of justification, then obviously you have not understood it. Justification by faith is not a legal myth which makes no difference to life. Indeed, twice in verses 19–20, Paul says that the gospel of Jesus Christ has meant the difference between death and resurrection to him. When someone receives the gift of God's grace in Jesus Christ, the old way of life dies and a new life is resurrected. 'I no longer live, but Christ lives in me.'

Herein lies the real glory of a genuine experience of God's grace in the gospel of Jesus Christ. It is not simply my turning over a new leaf, nor is it some legal fiction that I have been justified by God. Justification is never separated from the spiritual resurrection and a transformation that raises me into a newness of life.

This is basic Christianity.

This transformation, however, will not make us perfect. At our best, we are still sinners. But the glorious good news is that in you, if you are a justified sinner, the Lord Jesus Christ himself dwells. That is the one hope for people like us with all our frailties and all our weaknesses.

I am still by nature a lawbreaker, but in me there dwells the very Son of God who obeyed and kept the law of God in every detail. This is what Paul says: 'I live now by faith in the Son of God who loved me and gave himself for me. I live, yet not I, it is Christ who lives in me.'

And that is what the Christian life is – Christ living out his life, even in a justified sinner. To God be the glory and praise for such a gospel and for such a Saviour.

Jesus - you bring peace
to my inner man. To Actually
Believe its True is so
precious to me. I've been
so prideful, so rebellious
so wicked. you loved
me + gave yourself for
me. There is no other
Reason to live than
loving you + making
your name great!

8

SUBSTITUTION: AN EXPOSITION OF ISAIAH 52:13–53:12

SEE, MY SERVANT WILL ACT WISELY; he will be raised and lifted up and highly exalted. Just as there were many who were appalled at him – his appearance was so disfigured beyond that of any man and his form marred beyond human likeness – so will he sprinkle many nations, and kings will shut their mouths because of him. For what they were not told, they will see, and what they have not heard, they will understand.

Who has believed our message and to whom has the arm of the LORD been revealed? He grew up before him like a tender shoot, and like a root out of dry ground. He had no beauty or majesty to attract us to him, nothing in his appearance that we should desire him. He was despised and rejected by men, a man of sorrows, and familiar with suffering. Like one from whom men hide their faces he was despised, and we esteemed him not. Surely he took up our infirmities and carried our sorrows, yet we considered him stricken by God, smitten by him, and afflicted. But he was pierced for our transgressions, he was crushed for our iniquities; the punishment that brought us peace was upon him, and by his wounds we are healed. We all, like sheep, have gone astray, each of us has turned to his own way; and the LORD has laid on him the iniquity of us all.

He was oppressed and afflicted, yet he did not open his mouth; he was led like a lamb to the slaughter, and as a sheep before her shearers is silent, so he did not open his mouth. By oppression and judgment he was taken away. And who can speak of his descendants? For he was cut off from the land of the living; for the transgression of my people he was stricken. He was assigned a grave with the wicked, and with the rich in his death, though he had done no violence, nor was any deceit in his mouth.

Yet it was the LORD's will to crush him and cause him to suffer, and though the LORD makes his life a guilt offering, he will see his offspring and prolong his days, and the will of the LORD will prosper in his hand. After the suffering of his soul, he will see the light of life and be satisfied; by his knowledge my righteous servant will justify many, and he will bear their iniquities. Therefore I will give him a portion among the great, and he will divide the spoils with the strong, because he poured out his life unto death, and was numbered with the transgressors. For he bore the sin of many, and made intercession for the transgressors (*Isa.* 52:13–53:12).

FEW CHRISTIAN PEOPLE can read this passage without a profound sense of awe gripping their souls. It is dealing with matters that defy our understanding, or even our imagination. It describes in some accurate detail events which happened 800 years later: a preview, as it were, of the atoning death of Jesus Christ (described here as the Servant of the Lord), and how he became the Substitute for sinners.

This is the last of four servant songs in Isaiah. The first three are in chapters 42, 49 and 50. The fourth begins here in Isaiah 52: 13 with the words, 'Behold – Look – See my servant.' This is God the Father urging us to set our gaze on God the Son.

That is the only conclusion we can come to when we ask the question the Ethiopian Treasurer asked Philip the evangelist: 'Of whom does the prophet speak?' (*Acts* 8:34).

Almost every verse of this chapter is quoted in the New Testament. The issue of the identity of the Servant is decided for us when after the Upper Room Supper, Jesus says, 'It is written, "He was numbered with the transgressors", and I tell you that this must be fulfilled in me. Yes, what is written about me is reaching its fulfilment' (*Luke* 22:37). There is no doubt that Jesus' own answer to the question, 'Of whom does the prophet speak?' would be that the Suffering Servant of Isaiah is the sin-bearing Saviour of Calvary.

Notice that the Servant is not introduced first of all as Judah's servant to save them. He is first and foremost Jehovah's servant to fulfil his perfect will for the salvation of his people.

Now that pushes the horizons of our thinking back beyond the boundaries of time. The eternal Son of God who is the true servant of Jehovah is here depicted, long before he actually came into the world, engaging with God the Father in what the old divines would have called 'The Covenant of Redemption' between the Father and the Son.

In that Covenant, the Godhead plans out our salvation. The Father covenants his grace. The Son covenants his obedience as the Word made flesh even to the death of the cross. The Spirit covenants to apply to God's people all that the Son accomplished for them.

No one has drawn this picture more vividly than John Flavel, who exercised his ministry in seventeenth-century Dartmouth, Devon. He was held in high esteem by both Jonathan Edwards and George Whitefield. He puts it like this:

Here you may suppose the Father to say, when driving his bargain with Christ for you:

Father. My Son, here is a company of poor miserable souls, that have utterly undone themselves, and now lie open to my justice! Justice demands satisfaction for them, or will satisfy itself in the eternal ruin of them: what shall be done for these souls?

And thus Christ returns:

Son. O my Father, such is my love to, and pity for them, that rather than they shall perish eternally I will be responsible for them as their Surety; bring in all thy bills, that I may see what they owe thee; Lord, bring them all in, that there may be no after-reckonings with them; at my hand shalt thou require it. I will rather choose to suffer thy wrath than they should suffer it: upon me, my Father, upon me be all their debt.

Father. But my Son, if thou undertake for them, thou must reckon to pay the last mite, expect no abatements; if I spare them, I will not spare thee.

Son. Content, Father, let it be so; charge it all upon me, I am able to discharge it: and though it prove a kind of undoing to me, though it impoverish all my riches, empty all my treasures . . . yet I am content to undertake it.[1]

You get glimpses or hints of this in John 17:4, in the closing prayer of Christ's ministry among his disciples: 'Father, I have finished the work you gave me to do. Now Father glorify me with the glory I had with you before the world began.'

In the first and last stanzas of this song, it is clear that the servant of Jehovah is destined for unparalleled glory and honour. 'Behold my servant will act wisely. He will be raised and lifted up

---

[1] John Flavel, *Works* (1820 edition, repr. London: Banner of Truth Trust), 1968. vol. 1, p. 61.

and highly exalted' (52:13) And again in chapter 53:10: 'He will see his offspring, and prolong his days, and the will of the LORD will prosper in his hand.' Once more, the same motif appears at the end of the entire song: 'Therefore I will give him a portion among the great, and he will divide the spoils with the strong' (*Isa.* 53:12).

The Servant is the one who bears the glory of perfect manhood. The created order had not witnessed this since the fall of Adam and Eve into sin and the curse. Here is the last Adam, Jesus Christ, in all his perfection as the 'Proper Man', as Luther calls him. Now it is all the more astonishing and incredible that we should read: 'His appearance was so disfigured beyond that of any man and his form marred beyond human likeness' (*Isa.* 52:14). What is being described here for us is the grotesquely horrifying figure of a human being distorted and disfigured beyond recognition. This is further amplified: 'He had no beauty or majesty to attract us to him, nothing in his appearance that we should desire him' (*Isa.* 53:2).

Remember that this is the one whom angels and archangels admire and worship. He is the 'chiefest among ten thousand' and the 'altogether lovely' one of the Song of Songs (5:10, 16, KJV), and the bright Morning Star (*Rev.* 22:16).

In the light of all that, we must ask concerning this Servant, 'What produced such disfigurement and such deformity?'

There are basically two answers to the question.

There is *first* the human answer. 'He was despised and rejected by men, a man of sorrows and familiar with suffering. Like one from whom men hide their faces he was despised, and we esteemed him not' (*Isa.* 53:3). 'We considered him stricken by God, smitten by him and afflicted' (*Isa.* 53:4b).

In other words, men thought that he was suffering some ghastly retribution for his own sin. This is the ultimate blindness of which Paul speaks: 'The god of this age has blinded the minds of unbelievers, so that they cannot see the light of the gospel of the glory of Christ who is the image of God' (*2 Cor.* 4:4). They actually thought that the Servant was bearing the punishment of his own sin, and was stricken by God on that account. But this is categorically denied: 'He had done no violence, nor was any deceit in his mouth' (*Isa.* 53:9b).

That leads us to the *second* answer to our question – the *divine* answer.

It begins in verse 4 with a single word which is both a confident expression of truth and an appeal to reason: 'Surely . . .'

Handel's *Messiah* catches this note significantly in the chorus which repeats the word, 'Surely'. The word introduces a statement about the suffering and death of the Servant of Jehovah which clarifies in an unmistakable way the fact that he died in the place of sinners, as the perfect Substitute for our transgressions.

Professor R. A. Finlayson well described the words that follow as, 'An anatomy of sin and an anatomy of grace'[1] (*Isa.* 53:5). The prophet traces the nature of sin from the circumference to the centre. It is *transgression* (the outward act of breaking God's law), *iniquity* (the inward condition and disposition in our nature), *dispeace* (that is the dispeace which goes through our whole being from our mutiny against God) and *disease* (that is, the sickness which spreads to every area of our life and depraves us).

But then the prophet traces Christ's suffering in the same four steps from the circumference to the centre. He was 'pierced' or 'wounded' (the word refers to the outward assault on his body). Then he was 'bruised' (and that refers to the deeper pain or the hurt which human sin has caused). He further describes the nature of the Servant's suffering: 'upon him was the *chastisement*' that brought us peace. The NIV has *punishment*, but that is a bad translation. There is a great distinction between chastisement and punishment.

---

[1] Professor Finlayson used this expression in my hearing during an address given at the Strathpeffer Convention.

A stranger may punish, but only a father can chastise. Here the prophet is touching upon that deepest of all suffering which Christ endured when he uttered his cry of dereliction. Finally, he suffered *stripes*, which cut to the very quick of his being, under the Father's chastising hand.

Thus, what he bore perfectly matched our need as sinners. Ultimately what he bore was the wrath and judgment of a holy God. The Prophet thus sums it up: 'And the LORD has laid on him the iniquity of us all' (*Isa.* 53:6b). Calvin puts it precisely when he writes:

> This is our acquittal: the guilt that held us liable for punishment has been transferred to the head of the Son of God … he in every respect took our place to pay the price of our redemption.[1]

Luther sounds the very same note when he urges a friend to pray:

> Thou hast taken upon thyself what is mine and hast given to me what is thine.[2]

This truth of the substitutionary death of the Son of God in our place is the key which unlocks the deepest secrets of God's grace. It is also what makes it so serious to be outside of Christ: there is no shelter elsewhere from the storm of God's wrath. In the light of this, how glorious it is to have such a gospel to proclaim, expressed in Anne Ross Cousin's moving words:

> O Christ, what burdens bow'd Thy head!
> Our load was laid on Thee;
> Thou stoodest in the sinner's stead,
> Didst bear all ill for me.

[1] John Calvin, *Institutes of the Christian Religion*, trans., F. L. Battles, ed., J. T. McNeill (Philadelphia: Westminster Press, 1960), II. xvi. 5 and 7.

[2] *Luther: Letters of Spiritual Counsel* (London: S.C.M. Press), 1955, p. 110.

A victim led, Thy blood was shed;
Now there's no load for me.

The Holy One did hide His face;
O Christ, 'twas hid from Thee:
Dumb darkness wrapped Thy soul a space,
The darkness due to me.
But now that face of radiant grace
Shines forth in light on me.

Death and the curse were in our cup:
O Christ, 'twas full for Thee!
But Thou hast drained the last dark drop,
'Tis empty now for me.
That bitter cup, love drank it up;
Now blessing's draught for me.

It was pondering on these truths that caused the Apostle Peter to write: 'For Christ also suffered once for sins, the righteous for the unrighteous, that he might bring us to God' (*1 Pet.* 3:18).

Blessed be the God and Father of our Lord Jesus Christ for such a Saviour and for such a gospel!

9

SANCTIFICATION: 'CHANGED FROM GLORY INTO GLORY'[1]

*T*HIS SECOND SECTION OF THE BOOK is entitled 'The Salvation of God'. The salvation in view is salvation from sin. By God's grace this relates to our past (our guilt is taken away), to our future (we have an indestructible inheritance in heaven), and also to our present (God is presently and persistently at work in us to change us into the likeness of his Son). This is the present work of the Holy Spirit in our lives. Theologians often refer to it as 'sanctification', which simply means 'being made holy'.

One of Paul's most profound explanations of what this means is in 2 Corinthians 3:18 (ESV): 'And we all, with unveiled face, beholding the glory of the Lord, are being transformed into the same image, from one degree of glory to another. For this comes from the Lord who is the Spirit.'

There is one word which dominates this chapter of Paul's Second Letter to the Corinthians. It is the word 'glory'. It occurs twelve times, either as a noun or as an adjective, and twice in verse 18 alone. Our first task in studying this must be to seek to lay bare the real meaning of Paul's terms.

GLORY

Originally, the biblical word for glory in the Old Testament meant 'weight', in the sense of how heavy something was. It then

---

[1] This is a line from Charles Wesley's hymn, 'Love Divine, all loves excelling'.

came to signify someone's worth. (You may have heard some-one say, 'You're worth your weight in gold!') That referred to the character of the person. Paul makes the link between these two ideas in 2 Corinthians 4:17 (ESV) when he writes about 'an eternal weight of glory'.

The glory which is specifically God's would therefore be his character. He is worthy of praise and worship by his creation and his creatures because he is so great, so holy, so loving, and so pow-erful. In the New Testament the word for glory means the out-shining of an inward being or quality such as beauty or purity. In God, this radiance is so intense and the outshining so brilliant that it is overwhelming and unbearable for fallen humanity. Even the angelic beings in Isaiah 6 cover their faces in the presence of God's glory, and, in Acts 26:13, Paul tells King Agrippa that when the heavens opened on the road to Damascus, he saw a light brighter than the sun, and was struck to the ground.

It was in fact the exalted Christ he saw, and the vision blinded him. That was 'the glory of God in the face of Christ' (2 Cor. 4:6).

Where then is the glory of God to be seen? The Bible points us to FOUR places where God reveals his glory:

1. *In his creation.* 'The heavens declare the glory of God' (*Psa.* 19:1) 'The whole earth is full of his glory' (*Isa.* 6:3). That is in the inanimate creation. But in the creation of man, the Psalmist says to God, 'You . . . crowned him with glory' (*Psa.* 8:5).

2. *In his law.* This is what Paul has been explaining to us in 2 Corinthians 3:7–17. The law of God is a reflection of his character, which is why, as Moses carved the words of God's law into tablets of stone, his face became radiant with the glory of God, and the people could not look upon him (*2 Cor.* 3:7).

3. But there is something even more remarkable. God reveals his glory *in his Son*. When John describes the incarnation of the divine Word, Jesus Christ, he writes: 'We beheld his glory: the glory as of the only begotten of the Father' (*John* 1:14, KJV).

But there is something which even surpasses that in wonder:

4. The same God who has displayed his glory in creation, in the law and in his Son, purposes to display the same glory *in the lives of his people*. In 2 Corinthians 3:18, Paul tells us that the Holy Spirit is now labouring in the hearts and lives of God's people to display his glory in them, and to change them into his image.

However, there are two contrasts between the display of God's glory in the days of Moses and the display of his glory in his people under the new covenant.

The *first contrast* is indicated by the little word 'all' in verse 18. In the Greek it comes at the very beginning of the verse for emphasis. The point Paul is making is that the glory of the old covenant was *selective* (only Moses' face shone), whereas the glory of the new covenant in Christ is that it is *inclusive*: 'we . . . all'. That means that there is no redeemed child of God who is excluded; however weak, poor, despised by themselves or by others, every single one of us is embraced in this truth, and may say, 'This is my destiny by the grace of God.'

The *second contrast* is that, whereas Moses' glory was *fading* and *temporary* (verses 7, 11), the glory of which the gospel speaks is *increasing* and *permanent* (verses 11, 18).

Toplady expresses this as few others have done in his hymn, 'A debtor to mercy alone':

> The work which his goodness began,
> The arm of his strength will complete;

His promise is Yea and Amen,
And never was forfeited yet.

Things future, nor things that are now,
Nor all things below or above,
Can make him his purpose forgo,
Or sever my soul from his love.

FOUR VITAL PRINCIPLES

In the remainder of this chapter, I want to draw attention to four principles which Paul has embedded in 2 Corinthians 3:18 which clarify our understanding of *how* we are changed from one degree of glory to another.

1: THE WORK OF THE SPIRIT

First of all, the work of this inward transformation in the believer is accomplished in us by the Holy Spirit, the third Person of the Trinity. That means it is a divine work, not a human one. We cannot make ourselves like Christ. Paul says, 'For this comes from the Lord who is the Spirit.' So the great business of the Holy Spirit in the life of the Christian is to transform character, so that it may become radiant with the very glory of the Lord.

Ultimately, this is the most reliable evidence that the Holy Spirit indwells us. It is the fulfilment of our Lord's prayer in John 17:22, when he tells his Father, 'I have given them the glory that you gave me.'

2: LIKENESS TO CHRIST

Secondly, this transformation is a transfiguration into the likeness of Jesus Christ: 'We are being transformed into his likeness.'

The word for 'transformed' is the same word used in the Gospel account of Jesus' transfiguration, when his face shone like the sun. (*Matt.* 17:2). Significantly, Moses appeared on that mountain too.

I believe it is vital to press home the importance of this concept that the only reliable evidence of the Holy Spirit's work in the life of the believer is a *transformation of character*. Of course there are other evidences, such as gifts of various kinds, but the unique thing about the *fruit* of the Spirit is that it can never be counterfeited by the devil.

The devil can, apparently, produce counterfeits of all sorts of gifts, but never of the fruit of holiness of life. For it is this of which Jesus is speaking when he says, 'By their fruits you will know (or recognize) them' (*Matt.* 7:20). In Matthew 7:21–23, Jesus warns his disciples that no kind of successful service can ever be a substitute for convincing him that we truly know him. What counts is fruit in terms of a transformed character.

But I also think people often misunderstand what true Christlikeness is. They think holiness is a cold, stern, forbidding thing. But the fact is that there is a warmth and tenderness and naturalness and beauty about biblical holiness. One of the reasons for this lies in the perfect humanity of our Saviour. He is not only truly and perfectly God, he is truly and perfectly man. And a genuine work of grace makes us *more* human, not *less*, so that we are never more truly human and natural than when we are increasing in Christlikeness.

Do you know these words?

> Not merely in the words you say
> Not only in your deeds confessed
> But in the most unconscious way
> Is Christ expressed.

Is it a beatific smile,
A holy light upon your brow?
Oh no, I felt His presence while
You laughed just now.

For me, 'twas not the truth you taught,
To you so clear, to me so dim,
But when you came to me you brought
A sense of Him.

And from your eyes He beckons me,
And from your heart His love is shed,
Till I lose sight of you and see
The Christ instead.

That is the beauty of a restored humanity, and it is the reflection of the beauty of Christ. As William Still of Aberdeen once said, 'It is the spiritual thing done naturally, and the natural thing done spiritually, that marks the true man of God.'

3: THE MEANS

Thirdly, this work of changing us into the image of his glory is brought about by God-ordained means.

Paul uses a crucial phrase in this connection in verse 18. He says that it is in *'beholding the glory of the Lord'* that we are being changed or transformed into the same image. The NIV is, I believe, misleading at this point. It speaks of 'reflecting' rather than 'beholding', and reduces to a marginal reference the translation 'contemplate'. The ESV and KJV have the correct translation, 'beholding'. Others translate, 'gazing into'. The meaning is that as we behold the glory of the Lord, we are changed into his image.

Now the crucial question is: 'Where do we behold the glory of the Lord?' To enable us to understand this, let me summon the help of one of the greatest commentators on 2 Corinthians, Charles Hodge (who was one of the most distinguished professors in old Princeton Seminary). He says:

> [This beholding] is not the beatific vision of Christ which is only enjoyed in heaven, but it is that manifestation of his glory which is made in his word and by his Spirit.[1]

Thus, this transformation of the believer takes place as he gazes into the word of Holy Scripture, hears it expounded and taught, studies it for himself and absorbs its truth. This is what Holy Scripture is *for*. It is God's appointed means to change us into the image of his Son. And that is what sanctification is all about.

4: A LIFELONG WORK

Fourthly, this transformation is not the work of a day or a week or a year, but of a lifetime. It proceeds 'from one degree of glory to another' (*2 Cor.* 3:18, ESV). 'We are *being* changed' is the present continuous tense, which means that it is going on continuously. This change is always described in Scripture in horticultural and biological terms, such as birth and growth, sowing and reaping, pruning and fruit. Remembering this will save us from two dangers:

• *Discouragement with ourselves.* How easy it is for us to become discouraged and even distressed about our slow progress in the Christian way! We see others who always seem to be further on than ourselves, and we think, 'No one knows how pathetic my spiritual life is.' We need to speak to ourselves and say, 'I am being changed by God's grace; I am being changed so long as I keep gazing into God's Word.'

[1] Charles Hodge, *Commentary on 2 Corinthians* (1859; repr. London: Banner of Truth, 1959; repr. with *Commentary on 1 Corinthians* as one volume, 1974), p. 453.

- *Impatience with others.* Strangely enough, the two often accompany each other.

I am reminded here of something I noticed while at a conference in the U.S.A. at which I had been invited to speak. The hotel in which the speakers were accommodated was in the process of reconstruction. The result was that some walls only had plasterboard, electric cable snaked everywhere, and nothing was working normally. Then I noticed a sign which had been put up all over the hotel:

PLEASE BE PATIENT WITH US!
WE ARE BEING RENOVATED.

I thought, 'Me too! – That is true of everyone attending this conference!'

As I talked with many people during that week, I often thought of that sign, and asked God to give me, in my attitude to others, the patience he had extended to me so often.

This then is the sanctification of which the Bible speaks so much. It involves being changed. And this transformation is a work of the Spirit in us, in which we become more and more like Christ. It is the fruit of the working of God's Word in our lives. And it is a work of such magnitude that it continues throughout the whole course of our lives. That is why we need to be on our guard lest we be discouraged by its slowness, or become impatient with others whose progress is slow.

What a great word this is by which to live!

'We are being changed . . . from one degree of glory to another.'

> Finish then Thy new creation:
> Pure and spotless let us be;
> Let us see Thy great salvation,
> Perfectly restored in Thee;

Changed from glory into glory,
　　Till in heaven we take our place,
　Till we cast our crowns before Thee,
　　Lost in wonder, love, and praise.
CHARLES WESLEY

10

THE SECURITY OF
THE BELIEVER

WE LIVE IN A VERY SECURITY-CONSCIOUS AGE, when security
in all its forms – whether personal, industrial or national
security – has become a major industry. When I arrived
in Glasgow in 1977 as the minister of a city-centre church, we were
able to gain access to people's front doors with almost no barriers.
When I was retiring, twenty years later, it was impossible to get
beyond the security systems, physical, visual and audio, in order to
speak with the residents. Of course that is all a reflection of life in
an increasingly violent and dishonest society. But behind the physical insecurity it is very obvious that there is a deeper emotional and
personal insecurity which drives a remarkable number of people to
the doctor or the psychologist.

It is therefore highly relevant for us to consider the teaching
of Jesus in John's Gospel, chapter 10, verses 14–30, particularly as
he declares one of the deepest truths about his disciples in four
uncompromising words, found in verse 28: 'THEY SHALL NEVER
PERISH.' He then elaborates that truth in the next sentence, 'No-
one can snatch them out of my hand', and finally in verse 29 he
reinforces these statements with this: 'My Father, who has given
them to me, is greater than all; no-one can snatch them out of
my Father's hand.' That is Jesus' teaching on the security of the
believer, not just in this world, but right up to and after death, in
the world to come.

For every Christian, it is vitally important to have this assurance, based on Jesus' words, and for that reason, I would like to enquire into this passage with you.

The first thing to notice is that in the context of John 10, Jesus is answering two questions about those he calls 'my sheep'. He is of course speaking of himself as the perfect Shepherd who cares for his sheep, who are his disciples. The first question he deals with is, 'How can we recognize Christ's sheep?', and the second is, 'How can we know that they will never perish?' We will devote the rest of this chapter to these two questions.

1. HOW CAN WE RECOGNIZE CHRIST'S SHEEP?

There are – according to Jesus – four marks of Christ's sheep, or four evidences that they are truly his.

i. THEY HAVE SAVING FAITH.

In John 10:26, Jesus teaches this in a negative way in response to the Jews who had gathered around him in Solomon's Colonnade (verse 23). In verse 25 he diagnoses their problem in this way: 'You do not believe.' And then in verse 26 he says, 'You do not believe because you are not my sheep.' That is, the saving mark of the true disciple is personal faith in Jesus Christ. 'Saving faith', as Spurgeon put it, 'is the livery [or uniform] of the Lord's people.' So the mark of being one of the true sheep from Christ's flock is that we have personal, saving faith.

What does that mean? The best answer is given in the *Shorter Catechism* at Question 86: 'Faith in Jesus Christ is a saving grace, whereby we receive and rest upon him alone for salvation, as he is offered to us in the gospel.'

ii. *THEY LISTEN TO JESUS' VOICE.*

In verse 27, Jesus says, 'My sheep listen to my voice.' Earlier, in verse 3 of this chapter, Jesus gives this as the identifying mark of his sheep. You will notice that those who are truly Christ's sheep do not just *hear* his voice. Recently a strange distinction has entered the English language between 'hearing what someone is saying' and listening to a person, in the sense of accepting what is said. People will say, 'I hear what you are saying', but they are not agreeing with you. Now the true believer will never be a casual or careless or contrary listener to what Jesus is saying. This is the relation of the believer to the Word that proceeds from the mouth of God, Father, Son and Holy Spirit, and it is an identifying mark of Christ's sheep.

iii. *THEY ARE IN A UNIQUE RELATIONSHIP WITH JESUS.*

Jesus says in verse 27, 'I know them.' That truth is further spelled out in verses 14 and 15, where Jesus says, 'I know my sheep and my sheep know me – just as the Father knows me and I know the Father.'

We need to be clear that this is not a mere intellectual knowledge, nor is it concerned with acquiring information. It is the Divine Creator entering into fellowship with his creatures. It is the Divine Lover entering into fellowship with his beloved. Do notice where we are to learn the nature of this relationship. In verse 15 Jesus clearly elucidates the way in which the sheep know him and compares it with the way he and the Father know each other: 'Just as the Father knows me and I know the Father'. This is the deepest relationship which human beings can experience. It is of this that Scripture speaks when it describes faith as 'believing *into* the Lord

Jesus Christ', and when it uses 'knowing' as the verb to describe the marriage relationship of Adam and Eve (*Gen.* 4:1, KJV/ESV).

iv. *THEY FOLLOW JESUS.*

Leon Morris tells us that the present tense of the verb in verse 27b indicates a habitual following. It is, of course, the language of obedience. Luther puts it in this way: 'The sheep, though the most simple creature, is superior to all animals in this, that as soon as he hears his master's voice, he will follow no other.' So there is a distinctive direction about the lives of Christ's sheep. In verse 5, Jesus says, 'They will never follow a stranger; in fact, they will run away from him because they do not recognize a stranger's voice.'

That, then, is how you will recognize Christ's sheep: they have saving faith; they listen to Jesus' voice; they are in a unique relationship with him; and they live a life of seeking to follow him alone. Now we come to the second question, which is:

2. HOW CAN WE KNOW THAT CHRIST'S SHEEP WILL NEVER PERISH?

Again, there are *four reasons:*

i. *THE NATURE OF CHRIST'S DEATH FOR HIS SHEEP.*

In verse 15, Jesus says, 'I lay down my life for the sheep.' What Jesus is referring to, of course, is the nature of his death as a sacrifice for sinners. And the nature of that sacrifice is that it is *substitutionary.* He actually stood in my place and bore my condemnation. As we sing, 'In my place, condemned he stood, sealed my pardon with his blood.'

That is why there is now no condemnation for those who are in Christ Jesus. When Jesus died, he did not die to make salvation possible or potential, but to make it actual and effectual – he achieved it, and in doing so he paid the full price for sin and became the perfect Substitute for sinners. Thus the hymn writer asks us to sing:

> Payment God cannot twice demand,
> First at my bleeding surety's hand,
>   And then again at mine.

In that sense some of the most important words Jesus spoke on the Cross were, 'It is finished.' He completed the work of my salvation there, so that I am as surely saved today as I shall be on the Day of Judgment.

ii. *THE NATURE OF CHRIST'S GIFT TO HIS SHEEP.*

Verse 28a tells us, 'I give them eternal life, and they shall never perish.' Notice that eternal life is a GIFT. You cannot earn it like a wage, nor can you merit it like a reward. And notice that what he gives us is ETERNAL life. That of course is spiritual life, divine life. But if eternal life can cease, or if having been given it you can lose it, it cannot be *eternal* life, which by definition has no end. So, if God implants eternal life in your heart, it is there for ever.

iii. *THE NATURE OF JESUS' PROMISE.*

Verse 28b says, 'They shall never perish.' Now notice what Jesus is *not* saying. He is not saying that God's people will never be in trouble. He is not saying they will never stumble and fall. He is not saying they will never be harassed and hounded by their enemies. But he IS saying they will never perish. They are eternally secure. Backslide into a spiritual desert they may. Disobey God in a moment of folly they may. Fall into unfaithfulness to him they may. BUT PERISH THEY NEVER SHALL. Now that is not the promise or witness of a mere man. That is the word of the very Son of God himself, the Faithful and True Witness who cannot lie. It is the word of him who said, 'Heaven and earth may pass away, but my words will never pass away.' So let the heavens fall, let the earth remove, but his people will never perish.

iv. *THE NATURE OF THE UNITED COMMITMENT WITHIN THE GODHEAD FOR OUR SECURITY.*

There is a unity in the Godhead to which Jesus makes reference in verse 30: 'I and my Father are one.' Now, in this instance that unity is engaged in a combined determination to prevent Christ's sheep from perishing. 'No-one can snatch them out of my hand'; and, 'My Father . . . is greater than all; no-one can snatch them out of my Father's hand.' Notice the united work of the Father and the Son in our salvation. In verse 29, the Father gives us to the Son. The Son gives us eternal life by his death. And the Father and the Son have united hands, as it were, to ensure that we never perish. Thus the hands which formed the universe, and the hands that were pierced in bearing our sin, assure us that we can never doubt either the power or the love to save us to the uttermost.

It was told of an old Scottish minister that he was once visiting a very old, dying saint, who was still very conscious. Brown had known her well and was aware of her deep knowledge of God.

'Mary,' he asked her, 'what if at the last the Lord were to desert you?'

'Ah, minister, that would never be,' she responded, 'because, you see, He would lose far more than I.'

'How so?' asked the minister.

'Well,' she said quietly, 'I might lose my soul. But He would lose His honour, and that would never be.'

Do you see what she saw? Since God has vowed and covenanted that his sheep will never perish, what is ultimately at stake is nothing less than the very honour of God himself. On that we may securely rest for all eternity.

Augustus Montague Toplady completes his hymn, 'A debtor to mercy alone', with a wonderful statement of the truth we have been considering. Ponder these words carefully:

> My name from the palms of His hands
>   Eternity will not erase;
> Impressed on His heart it remains,
>   In marks of indelible grace.
> Yes, I to the end shall endure,
>   As sure as the earnest is given;
> More happy, but not more secure,
>   The glorified spirits in heaven.

Hallelujah!

11

GLORIFICATION: ATTAINING THE GOAL

ALVATION HAS THREE TENSES: past, present and future. All derive from the saving work of our Lord Jesus Christ, and all deal with some aspect of the spoliation that sin has brought into the world. The past involves salvation from sin's guilt and penalty. The present involves salvation from sin's power and dominion. The future involves salvation from sin's very presence. The first, roughly speaking, is justification. The second is sanctification. The third is glorification. The future dimension of Christian experience is our theme in this address.

The biblical perspective on glorification is magnificently highlighted in Romans, chapter eight. Here the apostle is encouraging the saints at Rome by speaking of the ministry of the Holy Spirit in bearing witness to our sonship in Christ. He begins, 'You received the Spirit of sonship. And by him we cry, "*Abba*, Father," The Spirit himself testifies with our spirit that we are God's children' (verses 15, 16).

WHAT ARE THE PROSPECTS?

There are endless privileges in being God's children. God has taken us, by nature children of wrath, and has raised us into the unspeakable dignity of being adopted children of God. God has only one begotten Son by nature; but he made us his adopted sons and daughters by grace. Moreover, he has raised us by grace into the same privileges that our Lord Jesus Christ enjoys now in the presence of the Father. This is what the apostle is glorying in. 'But,' he says, 'great and wonderful as these privileges are, there is something even more wonderful, and that is the future prospect of the children of God.' He leads us logically into that theme: 'If . . . children, then . . . heirs' (*Rom.* 8:17). That is one of the great aspects of redemption.

When people are looking for a job these days they frequently ask, 'What are the prospects? What of the future? What hope of advancement is there for me?' People leaving university are often going into dead-end jobs because of our economic situation, and the cry is, 'What are the prospects?'

That is one of the great questions of life. It does not matter who you are, one of the great issues before you is: 'What are the prospects? What of the future? What does it hold?'

Life is not going to go on forever. That is one of the fond dreams of modern man – that this life is going to go on forever as if it were some strange kind of perpetual dream. But it is not going to do that, and the great question we face is: 'What are the prospects?'

The Christian gospel answers this in a way that the world cannot. Paul is taken up with it. Part of the implication of being a child of God is that, by virtue of your sonship in Christ, a glorious inheritance beyond all description has been laid up for you by God. So when the Holy Spirit bears witness to you of your sonship, when you cry, '*Abba,* Father,' he is at the same time bearing witness to the fact that you are an heir of God and a joint-heir with Jesus Christ, and that the prospects are infinitely glorious for such people.

We find the same juxtaposition of thought in the apostle John, as he similarly exults in our sonship, saying, 'How great is the love the Father has lavished on us, that we should be called children of God! And that is what we are! . . . Dear friends, now we are children of God, and what we will be has not yet been made known.

But we know that when he appears, we shall be like him, for we shall see him as he is' (*1 John* 3:1–2).

Paul reminds us that we are saved 'in . . .hope' (*Rom.* 8:24; see also verse 20). He means that there is always a 'not yet' about the Christian's life in this world. This is an important thing for us to grasp, for the full description of salvation is not simply that we are saved by grace through faith. That is marvellously true, but it is only the beginning of the Christian's salvation. The full description is that we are saved by grace, through faith, *in hope*. We have not begun to see the Christian gospel in its fulness if we omit that hope of glory.

This means that while our trust is in the finished work of Christ and while we may sing about having full salvation here in this world, there is another sense in which our salvation is still to come. For the Christian, the best is yet to be. In the long term this is what distinguishes the Christian from the man or woman without Christ. For them, the worst is to come. For the child of God, the best is ahead. The last act in the drama of redemption is still to be performed, when God shall appear in the person of his Son in majesty and power to wind up the affairs of this bankrupt world. He will call mankind to appear before his judgment, and Jesus shall be the Judge.

That is why there are still so many tensions here. There are ongoing battles and struggles in our Christian experience, because we are living in the interim period between our salvation having been begun and the glory being consummated. In this age we groan within ourselves, waiting for the adoption, even the redemption of our bodies (*Rom.* 8:23).

PRESENT SUFFERING AND FUTURE GLORY

Paul's immediate purpose in urging this truth upon the believers at Rome is to give them a proper view of their trials, what he calls in verse 18 'our present sufferings'. He says that these 'are not worth comparing with the glory that will be revealed in us'.

Paul does not minimize the reality of the sufferings and trials of believers. Rather, he weighs them up accurately. He reckons with the full force of them. But, he says, there is something else to be reckoned with, and that is the glory God is preparing for his children, a glory so surpassingly wonderful that present sufferings cannot even be compared with it.

It is significant that the connection between suffering and glory is not just one of compensation. The glory actually grows out of the suffering of the believer. Paul expresses this in speaking of 'our light and momentary troubles'. He had already mentioned the tremendous pressure under which he served. But he says, 'Our light and momentary troubles are achieving for us an eternal glory that far outweighs them all' (*2 Cor.* 4:17). His point is that our union with Christ leads to both the suffering and the glory.

In Romans 8:17 there are three words which have the Greek prefix *sun*, together with. Paul says we are heirs *together with him,* that we suffer *together with him,* and that we will be glorified *together with him.* All are the outcome of our union with Christ. All are evidence that we are united with Christ. The glory flows out of the suffering, and the suffering is a guarantee of the glory to come.

WHEN WILL THIS BE?

There are three questions we need to ask about this glorification: *When will it take place? What is this glory* which shall be revealed in us? And *what difference should it make* to ordinary Christian people like ourselves, in the daily work to which God has called us, including some very difficult situations? What difference should this doctrine make?

We have a key to the answer to the first of these questions – When will this glorification take place? – in two places. First, in the phrase 'our present sufferings', literally, 'the sufferings of this present time' (*Rom.* 8:18, KJV). As Professor John Murray points out, 'present' is not simply a way of saying 'for the time being';[1] that is, we are having sufferings just now, but we will have glory later. It is almost a technical term for this present age in contrast to the age which is to come. The future age will be ushered in by the return of Christ. It is the age of the resurrection of the body. It is the day when the glory of the Lord and of his people will be revealed. The apostle is saying that time, which has already been bisected by Christ's first coming into the periods we designate BC and AD, will be bisected by the future coming of Christ in glory. That coming will usher in the new age, the age to come. The suffering of believers is in 'this present age'. The age to come is marked, not by our death, but by Christ's coming again in glory.

The other clue to the timing of our glorification is in verses 19–23, where Paul enlarges the scope of suffering to include creation. He says that the universe is involved both in the present suffering and in the future glory of the people of God. It is amazing to think of the way the sub-human creation shared in man's curse at the Fall but will be brought into glorious freedom with God's people.

God pronounced his judgment on Adam: 'Cursed is the ground because of you . . . It shall produce thorns and thistles for you' (*Gen.* 3:17–18). The creation is itself under judgment. The fall of man was not just the fall of humanity. It was the fall of the whole created order. Something happened that brought the whole creation into what Paul calls 'frustration' and 'decay'. So the creation is groaning together, waiting for the liberation of God's people.

The created order is not what it was when God formed it and saw that it was all very good. We see the decay. We see nature,

[1] *Commentary on Romans*, vol. I, p. 300.

as Alfred Lord Tennyson says, 'red in tooth and claw'[1] – the ugly cruelty of nature. We see what the poets grasped as the 'melancholy murmur' of the waves or the 'sighing' of the wind. There is a groaning through the whole of creation, a kind of symphony which speaks of the groaning of the people of God as they wait for the day of the liberty of God's children.

When the day of the Lord Jesus' appearing arrives, the creation will be involved in it, not just God's people. There will be a new heaven and a new earth in which righteousness will dwell. The trees of the field will clap their hands. The leaves of the tree of life shall be for the healing of the nations. And the animate creation will share in it too! Do you remember how the prophet Isaiah views it? 'The wolf will live with the lamb, the leopard will lie down with the goat . . . They will neither harm nor destroy on all my holy mountain, for the earth will be full of the knowledge of the LORD as the waters cover the sea' (*Isa.* 11:6, 9).

Paul says that 'the creation waits in eager expectation' (verse 19). But this is a weak translation. The language expresses the idea of someone standing on tiptoe – the kind of thing people do when they are waiting for somebody to arrive at an airport or a train station. There are crowds of people there. So when somebody is waiting for a friend, perhaps a fiancée, he is on tiptoe, peering over people, waiting. Then suddenly he catches a glimpse of that person. Or it is like people waiting on tiptoe for the dawning of a new day, as the psalmist notes. This is how creation is pictured. The whole cosmos is standing on tiptoe, groaning, waiting for the liberation of the glory of the people of God. That is what it will be, and the whole creation will be involved in it.

This is no small hole-and-corner affair we are involved in. When the redeeming grace of God comes to a man's life, it is no small thing. It is not limited to some small part of life. It involves the

1 Alfred Lord Tennyson (1809–92), *In Memoriam A.H.H.*, LVI.

entire creation. So we should set our hearts on that day and walk through this world as men and women who eagerly – like the creation itself which is here teaching us a lesson – wait for the day of God.

It needs to be underlined that this is not just the day of our death. That will be an entering into glory in one sense, and a glorious thing. 'To depart and be with Christ . . . is better by far' (*Phil.* 1:23). My mother, used to say, 'Sudden death, sudden glory!' And it is true, of course. Sudden glory is what the people of God experience at death. *The Shorter Catechism* says, 'The souls of believers are at death made perfect in holiness, and do immediately pass into glory' (*Q. & A.* 37). For those of us who have loved ones in glory, that is a great hope. But that is not the end of our hope. It is really just the beginning of it. The Christian hope does not focus on the immortality of the soul but on the resurrection of the body, and that is associated with Christ's appearing again. 'The blessed hope', of which Paul speaks, is 'the glorious appearing of our great God and Saviour, Jesus Christ' (*Titus* 2:13). This is the last stage in our adoption, and it is still to come. It is the day of glory, the day of Christ's return.

PARTAKERS OF CHRIST'S GLORY

What is this glory which shall be revealed in us? Since our glorification will be glorification with Christ, it shall be his glory. We really do not have any line to fathom the depths of this. All we are given to know is that this is the glory of the Lord Jesus Christ given to the believer. This is what he spoke of when he was praying to his Father: 'I have given them the glory that you gave me' (*John* 17:22).

It is in that sense that sanctification and glorification join together. God has given this glory to us, and the Holy Spirit is even now changing us from one degree of this glory into another

(*2 Cor.* 3:18). Holiness is glory begun below; glorification is holiness completed above. In the day of Christ all the glory of the Lord Jesus Christ will be the believer's. Have you grasped that? This is where we ought to do what the Psalmist does and say, 'Selah.' Pause and think about that. *All the glory of the Lord Jesus Christ will be the believer's!*

We know, of course, that while he was here on earth Christ's glory was veiled. As we sing at Christmas time, 'Veiled in flesh the Godhead see.'¹ But sometimes that glory broke through, and it is significant how it is described. Peter, James, and John caught a glimpse of it on the Mount of Transfiguration. The Gospel says of that incident, 'His face shone like the sun' (*Matt.* 17:2). Paul caught a glimpse of this glory on the road to Damascus, as he later told King Agrippa: 'About noon, O king, as I was on the road, I saw a light from heaven, brighter than the sun, blazing around me and my companions' (*Acts* 26:13). What was that light? It was Jesus.

'Who are you, Lord?' Paul asked.

'I am Jesus,' he said.

John also caught a glimpse of Christ's glory. He said it was 'like the sun shining' (*Rev.* 1:16). That is the Lord Jesus' glory. It is all we can grasp in this world. In that day, Jesus said, 'the righteous will shine like the sun in the kingdom of their Father' (*Matt.* 13:43).

We look forward to that day with sure and steadfast hope. For then our very bodies will be resurrected, and we shall be delivered from the very presence and stain of sin, freed from all its foul appurtenances, and liberated to share in the glorious consummation of all Christ has done. That will be far more wonderful even than man in his innocent state in the garden, when he bore the image of God. For then we shall bear the blinding glory of the Lord Jesus.

¹ From Charles Wesley's hymn, 'Hark! the herald angels sing.'

WHAT DIFFERENCE DOES IT MAKE?

Finally, what does such a glorious doctrine as this do for us as ordinary Christian people? Three important things.

First, it puts *meaning into history*. History is not cyclical. It is not merely going around in circles. It is linear. It is moving toward the day God has appointed for the end of the age and the ushering in of his glory. The doctrine of glorification tells us that God has not abdicated his throne. He is directing the course of this age until the day of the coming of his Son.

Second, it puts *heart into the sufferer*. All the trials of this present world are merely instruments in the hands of God to produce a glory in us beyond all comparison. These present groanings are even described by the apostle as the birth pangs of creation. 'We know that the whole creation has been groaning as in the pains of childbirth right up to the present time. Not only so, but we ourselves . . . groan inwardly as we wait eagerly for our adoption as sons' (*Rom.* 8:22, 23). Do you see this picture? Paul says our sufferings are a very special kind of suffering – the suffering of travail. This brings a new dimension into the Christian's experience of suffering, for it is not meaningless pain, but a productive pain – like a childbirth out of which glory will come.

Some years ago a missionary had been going through a time of darkness in his spiritual life. He went for a walk one day, and as he went through the bushes he saw something that caught his attention. It was the chrysalis of a butterfly on a branch. The butterfly was struggling to get out. And as he watched, the butterfly struggled and struggled. There was a tribulation going on. He thought he would help it. So he took his penknife and carefully slit the chrysalis. The creature came out. But he discovered that without the completed struggle it was only a deformed and broken thing. He learned at that moment that it was the tribulation that put glory into it.

Can you see your tribulations that way? They put heart into life. They form you. That is why the apostle can say, 'We know that in all things God works for the good' (*Rom.* 8:28).

This confidence does not appear as some naïve word of comfort. It derives from the theological consideration that those whom God foreknew, he also predestined, and those he predestined he also called, and those he called he also justified, and those he justified he also glorified (*Rom.* 8:29, 30). Said C. H. Spurgeon, 'Brethren, there is no stopping Him.' That is what puts heart into the sufferer.

Finally, it puts *hope into living*, because for the child of God the best is yet to be.

There was an old couple of whom I knew who lived in a little broken-down house in a Welsh valley. Their son was an architect who had done quite well in the city, and he began to make plans for his parents' old age. When he was free he used to come down and spread before them on the table the blueprint of a beautiful little bungalow that he was having built for them by the seaside. The old couple used to hear of this, and their eyes would light up just to think about it. The son left the blueprint with them, and as people came in they used to say, 'You must see what our son has prepared for us.' Then they would spread the blueprint out and explain, 'This is where the bedroom is, and this is the kitchen, and there's a little garden there.' One day the old lady said to one of her visitors, 'You know, sometimes we actually think we are living there.'

So it is with those who here have no continuing city but who seek one to come. We seek a city whose builder and maker is God, a city with foundations (see *Heb.* 11:10).

In a discussion of the incident at Bethsaida when Jesus touched the blind man's eyes, John Owen suggests that we see a parable within the miracle (*Mark* 8:22–26). Jesus asked, 'Do you see anything?' The man answered, 'Yes, a little, but not very clearly; I see men as trees walking.' Then Jesus touched him again, and he saw clearly. Owen says, 'Grace renews nature; glory perfects grace . . . Upon the first touch, his eyes were opened, and he saw, but very obscurely . . . But on the second, he saw all things clearly.'[1] Has this dawned on you yet? However glorious may be our experience of our Lord Jesus in this world, however much our hearts may have been lifted up in the joys of our Redeemer, we wait still for the second touch. That truly will be 'joy unspeakable and full of glory' (*1 Pet.* 1:8, KJV).

---

[1] John Owen, *Meditations and Discourses on the Glory of Christ* (1684), in *Works*, ed. W. H. Goold (1850–53, repr. London: Banner of Truth 1965), vol. 1, p. 383.

PART THREE
THE CHURCH OF GOD

12

THE PURPOSE OF
THE CHURCH

*T*HE CHURCH IS AT THE CENTRE of God's purpose in the world. It is the key both to world history and to biblical revelation. Moreover, the whole Godhead is involved in it. The Father chooses a people for himself. The Son dies to redeem that people. The Holy Spirit refines and beautifies them so that Christ may ultimately present them to himself, a glorious church, unspotted and unwrinkled.

The creation, calling and perfection of the church constitute the unifying theme of the Bible. So, in a sense, you cannot understand biblical religion unless you understand that at the heart of it lies this great purpose. With this in view – to understand God's purpose in the church – the apostle Peter can serve us as a guide and counsellor. He wonderfully unfolds his teaching in 1 Peter 2:4–10.

A PEOPLE FOR HIMSELF

There are many biblical metaphors for the church. Sometimes it is called God's family or household. On other occasions it is God's flock or Christ's body. On still other occasions it is described as Christ's bride whom he woos and draws to himself.

These images are varied and colourful, but it is not surprising that in his First Letter, Simon Peter chooses the metaphor of a building. After all, it was in response to his confession of faith at Caesarea Philippi (when Jesus asked, 'Who do people say the Son of Man is?' and Peter responded, 'You are the Christ') that Jesus told Peter, 'You are Peter, and on this rock I will build my church' (*Matt.* 16:13–18). Jesus was the one who first compared the church to a building, and it is in remembrance of this that Peter also speaks about the church as a building. God himself is the builder and Christ is the chief cornerstone. Thus, says Peter, 'As you come to him, the living Stone – rejected by men but chosen by God and precious to him – you also, like living stones, are being built into a spiritual house to be a holy priesthood, offering spiritual sacrifices acceptable to God' (*1 Pet.* 2:4).

Peter further elaborates on this picture in the verses that follow. He draws from Isaiah 28:16 and Psalm 118:22 to describe how God sets about building the church. The key, of course, is that Christ is the cornerstone of the building. He is God's chosen one, precious to him and also to those who believe on him. Isaiah 28:16 declares God's central purpose in history: 'I lay . . . in Zion, a chosen and precious cornerstone' (*1 Pet.* 2:6). Jesus is the beginning of God's new creation, the cornerstone of the new temple.

Peter also describes what happens when God lays Jesus Christ as the chief cornerstone of his church in this world: people are judged by their response to him. Those who believe on him become living stones themselves, built into this new temple. Those who reject him or cast him aside do not find that they bring him down. What happens, rather, is that he brings about their downfall. Jesus then becomes 'a stone that causes men to stumble and a rock that makes them fall' (*1 Pet.* 2:8).

Peter is reminding us that the only permanent body in the world is the church of Jesus Christ. Have you grasped that? Institutions, governments, and organizations will come and go, but the church of Jesus Christ will last to the very end.

Lord Reith was the first director-general of the British Broadcasting Corporation. He was a man who stood for righteousness and truth in a generation that was increasingly departing from them. One day he came into a committee room of the BBC where a number of the young *avant garde* were preparing a programme. 'We're preparing a programme about the church,' they said. 'We think it is high time that people in this advanced, technological generation recognize that the church is an anachronism. It belongs to past history. It is a curio. We are preparing a programme to discuss how we may give the church a decent burial.'

Lord Reith stood up to his full six feet five inches, looked down on them and said to the man who was most voluble, 'Young man, the church of Jesus Christ will stand at the grave of the BBC.'

And so it will! The church will stand at the grave of every human institution that has ever been or ever will be, because God has founded his church as the very centre of his purpose in history. The rest of history is, in a sense, the scaffolding within which God is building his church. One day that scaffolding will be taken away and then there will stand fully revealed this glorious purpose of God in preparing a people for himself.

We need to ask of this passage: What are God's purposes in building the church? How does Peter describe them? He gives three answers which are the thrust of the passage. God is building the church: first, for *worship*; second, for *fellowship*; third, for *evangelism*.

PURPOSE NUMBER ONE: WORSHIP

Worship is what 'offering spiritual sacrifices' refers to. 'You also,' he says, 'like living stones, are being built into a spiritual house [that is, a dwelling place for God] to be a holy priesthood, offering spiritual sacrifices acceptable to God through Jesus Christ' (*1 Pet. 2: 5*).

In the Old Testament, when God's people were a nomadic people, God gave them instructions for building a tabernacle, which served as a constant visible reminder to the people that God was in the midst of them. 'I will dwell among them', he said (*Exod.* 29:45–46).

When the Jews became settled in Jerusalem, God permitted them to build a temple for his glory. The significance of the temple was also that God dwelt among them. He did so in order that they might worship him – for his own glory.

But where is the temple of God now? Well, Peter says, *we* are the temple of God. True, the body of every one of us is the temple of the Holy Spirit, singularly (*1 Cor.* 6:19). But more especially, the people of God together are God's temple (*1 Cor.* 3:16–17). That is where he dwells in order that we might offer him acceptable sacrifices or spiritual worship. That is the point of the church's existence.

Let me emphasize one or two things about this. First, worship is *primary,* in terms of importance. If you ask, 'What is the great business of the church in this world? What is its great calling by God?' – this is the answer: The purpose of the church of Jesus Christ is *worship.* This will be the continuous activity of the church in its perfect form in heaven, because there, day and night, they cry, 'Worthy is the Lamb, who was slain, to receive power and wealth and wisdom and strength and honour and glory and praise' (*Rev.* 5:12). They are taken up with the worship of God. This is the church's great business here too. When God builds a temple he builds it primarily that he might have worshippers.

Recall how Jesus spoke to the woman of Samaria when she tried to divert him from the issues he was touching in her life. She said, 'Our fathers worshipped on this mountain, but you Jews claim that the place where we must worship is Jerusalem.' But Jesus replied: 'Neither on this mountain nor in Jerusalem . . . the true worshippers will worship the Father in spirit and truth' (*John* 4:20–23). That is how God is to be worshipped.

But notice what Jesus also said: The Father seeks such worshippers (verse 23). God was seeking that woman, sending the Lord Jesus Christ to the well – and her to the same well to meet him. That is the whole point of the incident. When Jesus sought that woman he was seeking a worshipper.

What, then, secondly, about the *nature* of worship? Peter says that it is *spiritual* rather than mechanical. That is, it engages the heart as well as the lips and the mind. Worshippers must worship the Father in spirit and in truth. This is why we need to be careful that we do not fall into the danger that Jesus identified in the case of the Pharisees: 'Well did Isaiah prophesy of you, when he said, "This people honours me with their lips, but their heart is far from me"' (*Matt.* 15:7–8, ESV). Of all divorces, this is the most fatal – the divorce of the lips from the heart in worship. God wants spiritual worship: not a mere outward performance, but the engagement of heart, mind, will and every faculty to exalt and praise him.

Thirdly, what is the *test* of true worship? Peter speaks of 'offering spiritual sacrifices *acceptable to God*' (*1 Pet.* 2:5).

How do you assess whether worship is real worship or not? Well, says Peter, the test is this: 'Is it acceptable to him?' The problem, you see, is that so often in our thinking worship is tested by whether it is 'acceptable to *me*'. People say, 'I didn't get much out of that.' But it is not *what I get out of worship* that is the vital thing; it is *what God gets out of it*, because the thing that worship ought to focus on is what is pleasing to him. That is the real issue in biblical, spiritual, God-centred worship.

The great Puritan, Stephen Charnock, wrote of worship: 'When we believe that we ought to be satisfied rather than God glorified, we set God below ourselves . . . as though we were not made for him but he hath a being only for us.'¹ That is true. So the great aim of worship is that God's people should be taken up with God. That

¹ *The Existence and Attributes of God*, Baker edition, vol. 1, p. 241.

involves the whole of life, because worship is giving glory to God in every sphere of life. You cannot worship like that on Sunday unless you are living like that from Monday to Saturday.

PURPOSE NUMBER TWO: FELLOWSHIP

The second purpose of the church is embedded in 1 Peter 2:4–5. As we come to Christ we are built together like stones in a building; that is, our union with Christ carries with it a union and sharing with each other.

That leads us to consider the *nature of fellowship*. The root idea of fellowship in the New Testament is that we have something in common. That is what the word means: *sharing in common*. What the stones in the building have in common is their relationship to the head cornerstone; but they cannot be joined to him without being joined to one another. So true Christian fellowship is a sharing of Christ as our most glorious common possession.

One of the reasons that alienation is such a problem in the modern world is that it is natural to us as sinners. What we need to discover is that our real alienation is not from one another. It is alienation from God. But the answer to alienation is fellowship: sharing with God the Father, God the Son and God the Holy Spirit, and sharing with one another. When we are having fellowship with one another, we ought to be sharing what we have come to know of God, and we ought to allow others to share what they have come to know of God with us. It is a sharing in both directions with each other. Have you ever noticed Paul's memorable little phrase in Romans 1:12? He wants to go to Rome, 'that you and I may be *mutually* encouraged by each other's faith'. The great apostle expressed his deep need to be encouraged by others. So also should we be encouraged mutually by other Christians' faith.

There are two dimensions to this fellowship. The *vertical* dimension is with the Godhead through Christ. The *horizontal* dimension is with the people of God, also through Christ. A true work of grace brings us into both these dimensions, and the church is where they are to be cultivated. Fellowship with God is the fountain of our fellowship with one another, and true fellowship with one another leads always to a deepening of fellowship with the Father and the Son.

That leads us to consider the *significance of fellowship*. If its nature is that it is a *work* of grace, and that God creates it, its significance is that it is a *means* of grace: God uses it for his purpose. A mutual sharing of Christ with each other in the company of God's people is not an optional extra in the Christian's life. It is not a luxury that is added, nor a kind of postgraduate class for the gifted. Fellowship belongs to the essence of our new life. It is one of the means of grace that God has provided for the upbuilding of his church and the glorifying of his name.

Since God has purposed that our fellowship with him be nourished by our fellowship with each other, we dare not ignore this great tool of his for building the church. Indeed, the New Testament warns us about neglecting to meet together and urges us to consider how to stir up and encourage one another. The Apostle John even tells us that fellowship is a test of life. He says, 'If we walk in the light . . . we have fellowship with one another' (*1 John* 1:7).

So fellowship in a church is not just a cultural thing. People often say to me, 'Oh, we Scots are rather retiring, you know; we don't find it easy to give ourselves to one another.' I say, 'This is not a cultural matter. It is the essence of what God creates when he draws us to himself.'

The reason he does it is that true fellowship begins when we are released from a preoccupation with ourselves and are given a concern for other people, a love for them that is the love of Jesus reaching out through us.

True fellowship has its deepest significance in what it leads to, and that is fellowship with God. This is what we are concerned with as we share fellowship with one another, that our fellowship with him may be deepened and increased. When fellowship is pursued for its own sake it turns sour. Its end, like worship, is the glory of God, and heaven will be its perfection.

PURPOSE NUMBER THREE: EVANGELISM

Peter further expresses the purpose of the church when he writes: 'But you are a chosen people, a royal priesthood, a holy nation, a people belonging to God, that you may [here is God's purpose in constituting them a people and choosing them] declare the praises of him who called you out of darkness into his marvellous light' (*1 Pet.* 2:9). The verb translated declare is *exangello*, which means to tell out or proclaim. That tells us that God's third purpose in creating the church is *evangelism*.

Peter piles up the privileges of God's people here, calling them 'a chosen people, a royal priesthood, a holy nation, a people belonging to God'. These are great honours. But the higher the privilege, the greater the responsibility. And so he moves from saying, 'you are', to saying, 'that you may'. 'You are' these things in order 'that you may declare the glory of him who has called you out of darkness into his marvellous light.' Hidden in these descriptions of the church is a solemn warning. It is the warning that Israel, as God's chosen people, holy nation and royal priesthood, did not live up to these privileges. God did not give them these blessings in order that they might consume them upon themselves. He did not create this royal priesthood, this holy nation, for its own sake. But the people became absorbed with their privileges. They heard the 'you are', but they were deaf to the 'that you may'. They did not listen to God when he told them that he had given them these privileges that they might be a light to the Gentiles and a blessing to the world.

Do you know why Jesus cleansed the temple? Was it because he saw the commercialization of the temple precincts? That was part of it, of course. But it was more than that. Where was this buying and selling going on? It was in the court of the Gentiles. That is where they were buying and selling – the very place God had designed for the Gentiles, so that they might come to learn how to approach God, how to receive him, how to pray that they might be given the light they needed. Jesus' greatest indignation was because the Jews had become careless about the souls of these people.

Two things should be noted here by way of conclusion.

Evangelism, this passage suggests, is the proclamation of the deeds of him who brings us from darkness to light. It is pointing to what God has done. 'Declare' implies speaking – preaching, talking, sharing – however you may describe it. But there is another form of evangelism described here: 'Live such good lives among the pagans that, though they accuse you of doing wrong, they may see your good deeds and glorify God on the day he visits us (*1 Pet.* 2:12). That is the evangelism of a distinctive, God-orientated life. It is evangelism which causes others to say, not, 'Look, what a splendid person that is', but rather, 'How great is that person's God.'

That is what Jesus spoke of when he said, 'In the same way, let your light shine before men, that they may see your good deeds and praise your Father in heaven' (*Matt.* 5:16).

Notice, too, evangelism's motive. It is that others may 'glorify God on the day he visits us' (*1 Pet.* 2:12). The glory of God is the end of everything in the church, and it is nowhere more so than in evangelism.

If you think of it, the ultimate motive of evangelism is not found anywhere else than here. What sends men to the other side of the earth in Christ's name is that there is some place where God is being robbed of his glory. What sends us into a world that is desperately sick (although it does not know it) is that the world is living for, worshipping and serving the creature rather than the Creator, and God is being robbed of his glory there. To restore that glory is both the fundamental motive of evangelism and its ultimate goal.

13

MINISTRY IN
THE CHURCH

*T*HE THEME OF MINISTRY IN THE CHURCH has come to the forefront of people's thinking recently. There was a time when the great obsession was with the unity of the church. But if I judge rightly, in recent days there has been a ferment of writing and thinking about ministry, usually focusing upon warnings against the danger of a few monopolizing ministry, and advocating the every-member ministry which Scripture insists upon.

We do well in this context, to be guided by Scripture, and particularly that classic passage on ministry, Ephesians 4:7–16:

> To each one of us grace has been given as Christ apportioned it. This is why it says, 'When he ascended on high he led captives in his train and gave gifts to men' (What does 'he ascended' mean except that he also descended to the lower, earthly regions? He who descended is the very one who ascended higher than all the heavens, in order to fill the whole universe.) It was he who gave some to be apostles, some to be prophets, some to be evangelists, and some to be pastors and teachers, to prepare God's people for works of service, so that the body of Christ may be built up until we all reach unity in the faith and in the knowledge of the Son of God and become mature, attaining to the whole measure of the fulness of Christ. Then we will no longer be infants, tossed back and forth by the waves, and blown here and there by every wind of teaching and by the cunning and craftiness of men in their

deceitful scheming. Instead, speaking the truth in love, we will in all things grow up into him who is the Head, that is, Christ. From him the whole body, joined and held together by every supporting ligament, grows and builds itself up in love, as each part does its work.

Three basic themes dominate this passage. First, the *origin* of true ministry. Second, the *nature* of true ministry. Third, the *goal* of true ministry.

THE ORIGIN OF TRUE MINISTRY

Essentially, all true ministry in the church derives, like everything else in the believer's life, from God. That is the foundation upon which Paul builds everything. 'To each one of us grace has been given' (*Eph.* 4:7). This means that the ultimate origin of all ministry is in the grace of God.

Here the apostle Paul is probably not so much emphasizing the saving grace which achieved our redemption as the serving grace which enables us to engage in ministry. For whatever ministry we exercise, it is a gift of God's grace. That is a foundation upon which we need to be firmly built, a ground into which we need thoroughly to be rooted if our thinking about ministry is to be accurate and our practice of ministry is to be glorifying to God. Our ministry will never end in the glory of God if we have not established clearly that it begins in the grace of God.

That is why the word 'gift' is used. Every ministry is a gift. Therefore, no one should feel inflated with a sense of his or her own importance. We receive gifts, and gifts magnify the Giver, not the exerciser of the ministry.

Grace is distributed by the Lord Jesus Christ from his ascended glory: 'To each one of us grace has been given as Christ apportioned it. This is why it says: "When he ascended on high, he led captives in his train and gave gifts to men"' (*Eph.* 4:7–8).

Paul here pictures the Lord Jesus as having ascended to the Father's presence, carrying the spoils of victory with him and then distributing his *largesse* to his people.

Psalm 24 is the classic Old Testament reference to this triumph. The psalmist cries, 'Lift up your heads, O you gates; be lifted up, you ancient doors, that the King of glory may come in' (*Psa.* 24: 7).

The cry comes back from the ramparts of heaven, 'Who is this King of glory?' (verse 8).

And as the Lord Jesus is borne up into the upper regions of heaven, the people cry, 'The LORD strong and mighty, the LORD mighty in battle . . . he is the King of glory' (verses 8–10). He, back from his victorious battle with the powers of darkness, then begins to distribute gifts to his people – to give them a ministry.

The apostle sees a picture of this in Psalm 68:18, from which he quotes: 'This is why it says, "When he ascended on high, he led captives in his train and gave gifts to men"' (*Eph.* 4:8).

The wording in Psalm 68:18 may seem to be saying something rather different from what the apostle says here. It says, he '*received* gifts from men.' However, the Hebrew word can be translated 'bring' as well as 'receive', and the apostle is using the first meaning as he applies the Psalm to the Lord.

So the *first* great lesson is this: all true ministry in Christ's church *derives* from Christ's ministry. He is the true minister of the tabernacle (*Heb.* 8:2). He is the shepherd and overseer of our souls (*1 Pet.* 2:25). He is the apostle and high priest of our profession (*Heb.* 3:1). He is the *diakonos* of the circumcision for the truth of God (*Rom.* 15:8). All the great titles that are used for our ministry are first applied to Jesus. So it is the ministry of the Lord Jesus Christ which is continuing in his church.

He who began his ministry here in this world continues it, as Luke tells us at the beginning of Acts: 'All that Jesus *began* to do and teach.' He told us what Jesus did in the Gospel; now, in the

Book of Acts, he describes what the ascended Christ continues to do through the gifts of ministry he gives us. In that sense all true ministry derives from him.

The *second* implication is that all true ministry in the church *reflects* Christ's ministry. That needs to be explained. Paul adds (after the quotation from Psalm 68) that the Christ who ascended to glory is also the Christ who descended to the lowest regions (*Eph.* 4:9–10).

The early fathers laid that alongside the difficult reference in 1 Peter 3:19 about Christ preaching to the spirits in prison, and suggested that it referred to Jesus visiting Hades. I think it more likely that Paul is reminding us of the same truth he sets before us in Philippians 2:5–11, namely, that the ministry of the Lord Jesus was an astonishing example of self-humbling obedience to the ultimate point of death, even the death of the cross.

Our ministry is to reflect his, not in terms of its redeeming accomplishments but in terms of its self-humbling. Jesus' servant ministry is to be our pattern. This means that the essence of ministry is not office but service. It is not self-display but self-denial. This needs to be impressed deeply into our thinking. The essential element of ministry is that it reflects the servant attitude of Jesus. All forms of ministry need to conform to it.

THE NATURE OF TRUE MINISTRY

Notice, *first*, that it is marked by *diversity*. It is obvious that Ephesians 4:11 mentions only a small selection of the various ministries described in the New Testament. 'He gave some to be apostles, some to be prophets, some to be evangelists, and some to be pastors and teachers.' There are three main places in the New Testament where we have a list of gifts of ministry. This is one. The other two are Romans 12:6–8 and 1 Corinthians 12:28. But even these, put together, are probably not intended to provide a comprehensive list.

We are all called to exercise a ministry. Ministry is the universal privilege of God's people. But there are characteristics about this specific list that have special significance.

For example, this list forces us to think about office as well as ministry in the church.

A few paragraphs ago I underlined that the essence of ministry is not office but service. I am not now contradicting that. I want instead to hold both of these together and say that, although the essence of ministry is not office, there is such a thing as an office to which some are appointed because of the ministry they exercise.

The word 'office' scarcely occurs in the New Testament. When Paul says that he magnifies 'his office' (Rom. 11:13, KJV) he literally means his 'ministry' (the Greek word is *diakonia* which is related to the word for deacon). But there is no doubt that the idea of some being appointed to positions of authoritative leadership in the church is clearly present in the New Testament. The church is not an unstructured organism. It is structured. Moreover, it is an organization as well as being an organism. So we may rightly speak of the *office* of apostle, the *office* of elder, and so on.

The apostle was chosen by Jesus Christ, and there were certain qualifications he met. He had to have been an eyewitness of the risen Lord (*1 Cor.* 9:1). It is upon the apostles that the church is built in a doctrinal sense: 'the *foundation of the apostles* and prophets, with Christ Jesus himself as the chief cornerstone' (*Eph.* 2:20). By definition this was a distinct and a temporary office. True, there is an apostolic ministry in a wider sense of the word, in the sense of Christians being sent by God to do his work. In that sense we are all apostles ('sent ones'). But in the strict sense, the office of apostle was for a short time only. Today the apostles minister to us through the pages of Holy Scripture alone.

The prophets also had a clear position in the early church. They differed from the apostles in that their inspiration was occasional and their authority was therefore subordinate. Nevertheless, they were vehicles of direct revelation. In Ephesians 2:20 Paul brackets them with the apostles as the foundation of the church, and in Ephesians 3:5 he portrays them as being recipients of new revelation. This 'was not made known to men in other generations as it has now been revealed by the Spirit to God's holy apostles and prophets.' John Stott speaks well and rightly when he says that as the foundation on which the church is being built the prophets have no successors any more than the apostles have, for the foundation was laid and finished centuries ago, and we cannot tamper with it.[1]

The gift of evangelist is difficult to define. It probably refers to those who were commissioned to preach the gospel where it had not previously been known. William Barclay thinks of evangelists as missionaries of the early church. This was a ministry to which they were called.

The double expression 'pastors and teachers' seems to be a description of one ministry, 'the pastors who are teachers'. Moreover, their ministry is basically the same as that of the New Testament elder, because the calling of the elder in the New Testament church is to do precisely what the pastor or teacher also appears called to do. An elder is to shepherd or pastor God's flock (*Acts* 20:28; *1 Pet.* 5:2–4). An elder is to be gifted in teaching (*1 Tim.* 3:2). So pastors and teachers are to be found among those who are described as elders in the church.

Here, I believe, we need to preserve the true balance of Scripture. In Britain, at least, the concern to emphasize the truth that we all have a ministry has clouded two vital issues. One is the need

---

[1] John R. W. Stott, *God's New Society: The Message of Ephesians* (Leicester: IVP), 1971, p. 107.

for the church to be ruled and led. The other is the need for the church to be taught and fed by God.

The function of the elder-pastor or elder-teacher is to oversee or lead the flock of God. The manner of this oversight is controlled by the idea of the origin of ministry. Ministry originates in the grace of God, so it has to be done in the attitude of Jesus – not with lordly ambition but as being examples to the flock, in lowly service (*1 Pet.* 5:3). That kind of oversight is needed in the church. And where it exists the command is to 'obey your leaders and submit to their authority' (*Heb.* 13: 17). We need to acknowledge this in a day when it is so common to dismiss or discount authority.

The church is not a democracy. There is a tendency for us to imagine that democracy somehow holds a favoured place with God. But the church is not a democracy, the rule of the majority. The church (if anything) is a theocracy and even a monarchy; that is, it has Christ as its king and head.

The New Testament tells us that God has delegated authority. In the state he has delegated it to rulers. In marriage he has delegated a certain authority to husbands. In the church he has delegated authority to those who are overseers. They are to be obeyed in the Lord.

Today professing Christian people are frequently not associated with any body of local Christian people but go here and there at a whim. People sometimes tell me, 'I don't belong anywhere. I don't associate myself with any one body. I just go wherever the Lord leads me.' I put this question to them: 'To whom, then, do you submit?' That is an important question, because God has appointed pastors as shepherds over the flock and has given the responsibility of ruling to them (*Heb.* 13:17).

The other function of the pastor is to feed, or teach, the flock. In that connection I think it is highly significant that the ministries described by Paul in Ephesians 4:11 are all teaching ministries. The apostles and prophets are the foundation; they wrote the doctrines. Evangelists proclaim the truths to those who have not heard them. Pastors and teachers expound the texts and instruct from them.

Again, let me apply this to the contemporary situation. In our eagerness to get away from the one-man ministry model we sometimes get caught up in a tendency to devalue biblical preaching. People meet to share, discuss, dialogue or – and this is particularly subtle – 'just to worship'. People say, 'We don't meet as you do; we just meet to worship' – as if the preaching of the Word of God is in some sense separable from worship. But what *produces* worship is the careful exposition of the Word of God in the power of the Holy Spirit. That is what glorifies God, sets him before the hearts and minds of men, makes us bow down before him and magnify his glory, and honour him for all he has wrought for us in Jesus Christ. *That* produces worship. Not only so, but according to Paul, this is also the thing that in turn strengthens Christians in general to minister and employ the gifts Christ has given to them. In other words, the ministry of the preached Word is not an alternative to every-member ministry but is the very thing which makes it possible.

THE GOAL OF TRUE MINISTRY

What, then, is the purpose of the ministry? Notice how Paul tells us that the purpose of this ministry is to prepare God's people for ministry (*Eph.* 4:12). In other words, ministry is not a thing or an end in itself; it is a means to an end. And the end to which it should lead is the equipping of God's people for works of service. It is to bring them into the condition God means them to be in as his people, enabling them to minister.

Note Paul's verbal build-up in verse 13. The Lord Jesus Christ ascended to distribute gifts to all his people within the church. He has distributed the gifts of the ministries of the Word, which are central, in order to equip God's people that they might be enabled to minister. That will continue until we reach 'the whole measure of the fulness of Christ'. The Lord said, 'I will build my church.' Here, through Paul, Jesus lays down plans for building and maturing the church through its members' ministry.

This means setting us free from self-interest so that the focus of our concern will not be upon ourselves, but upon the building up of the body. Is that one reason why the ministry of the Word is at the centre of the apostle's thinking? If one of the things that prevents us from ministering to one another is self-absorption and self-centredness, then the ministry of the Word sets us free from that to minister to one another.

Many who are called to pastoral ministry are threatened by the ministry of fellow believers. So we set limits to the kind of people we will allow to minister to us. How mistaken! There is an endless variety of ministry that God raises up in a congregation, and this ministry is totally mutual. Moreover, the ministry of the Word ought to provoke and increase it. Those who are involved in the ministry of the Word as pastors and elders should pray for it.

It is in this context that it will be clear why it is a disturbing thing when our focus is upon the more exciting and spectacular gifts and so little upon the ministries of helping and encouraging, contributing and serving. It is an alarming thing if we are interested in the more attention-gaining ministries! Could that be because the servant nature of ministry has been something about which we have not really allowed God to teach us?

Paul brings his teaching here to a climax by noting that, as we minister to one another, *three marks* will be seen in God's people: *unity* ('until we all reach unity in the faith and in the knowledge of the Son of God'), *maturity* ('and become mature') and *conformity* ('attaining to the whole measure of the fulness of Christ,' verse 13). Our concern should be that we might experience through our mutual ministry to one another within the church that unity, maturity and conformity to him that are the marks of true church life.

Furthermore, *two elements* in the church's life will keep us from becoming victims of the latest theological fad ('blown here and there by every wind of teaching') or the latest novel idea ('by the cunning and craftiness of men in their deceitful scheming,' verse 14). They are *truth* and *love* working in harmony.

Truth and love need to be held together. Neither must be emphasized at the expense of the other, nor must one be evacuated of the other. Truth and love need each other, and it is the truth in love that will keep us from falling into the dangers of which verse 14 speaks.

In the end, what flows from Christ returns to Christ. He gave gifts that he might gain glory. Thus Paul says, 'Instead, speaking the truth in love, we will in all things grow up into him who is the Head, that is, Christ. From him the whole body, joined and held together by every supporting ligament, grows and builds itself up in love, as each part does its work' (*Eph.* 4:15,16). This is every-member ministry. It is every part fulfilling its function – not trying to fulfil somebody else's function but fulfilling its own function. The eye, then, does not look upon the hand and regard it as inferior, nor the foot upon another limb and regard it as superior to itself. There is none of this in the body of Christ when it is working properly. Every part is released for this sole purpose: that the body of Christ may grow and build itself up in love.

Are you impressed by how much the apostle speaks of the central place of love in this ministry? What prevents us from ministering to one another is lack of love. The opposite of the New Testament word for love is not hatred but self-love. And the reason we are not set free to minister to each other and serve one another is often because we are absorbed with ourselves rather than with a love for our brethren.

Supremely, however, the apostle says that the great motive for ministry is a desire for the glory of God. All ministry comes from him as the head, and all ministry goes back to him as the goal to which we aim. 'Each part working properly' means that each part is at the disposal of the head. Instructions come from the head. The body is disordered when the head sends a message to the hand to do something and the hand does not respond. But when the hand is at the disposal of the head, then it fulfils the function for which the head intends it. That is really the key to true ministry: whether we are at the disposal of the head for whatever function he has for us within his body.

We need to bring it down to this issue. Are we then – are you in particular – at the disposal of the head in order that everything may find its goal in him and his glory? That is the patern on which God's church is built.

14

GOD'S FELLOW-WORKERS,
OR, FOUR LAWS FOR
CHRISTIAN SERVICE

OUR TITLE IS DRAWN FROM PAUL'S WORDS in 1 Corinthians 3:9. This chapter is, of course, the passage where Paul deals with some of the misunderstandings which had arisen in the church at Corinth about the nature of the work of God, and of the ministry of the Word.

There were some very profound misunderstandings, obviously, and disorders too, in the church in Corinth. It is interesting, is it not, how we so often think of the apostolic church as being the idyllic and ideal trouble-free situation? We often speak somewhat unrealistically about apostolic days and 'the apostolic church'. It is very obvious that Paul was dealing with some of the very issues that you and I are dealing with (alas) in our own fellowships: factions and squabbles; people not getting on with each other; or not getting their place; broken marriages; lowering standards in the church; things being accepted in the church which are very obviously distressing; disorder in the exercise of gifts; criticism and slander.

All this was there in Corinth already; and it just shows that there is no ideal spot in which to serve God or to minister the Word, except the one where he has set us down. That is the ideal place in the world to minister, and we need to be persuaded of this, because so often what niggles away at the back of our minds is, 'If

I was just there, instead of here, everything would be all right. If I were in his place, I would not be in this mess; but I am here.' The simple fact is there is no ideal place in which to minister the Word, or to serve God, except the place where he has put you. That is why it is so very important to know that you are in the place of God's calling. Then you can say, 'It was God who called me and placed me here. This was the place of his perfect choice for me, and here I shall stay, by his grace, until he moves me elsewhere.

In this passage, there are four things which emerge which we might call *Four Laws for Christian Service*. The first of them could be put in some form such as this:

GOD'S PRIMARY CONCERN IS WITH THE WORKER, RATHER THAN THE WORK.

God's preoccupation is not with our service but with our character. That seems to me to lie behind at least the first four verses of 1 Corinthians 3. The reason the Corinthians did not grasp what the service of God was all about, or the principles on which it was based, was because they were 'carnal' rather than 'spiritual'.

Notice the language here. Paul does not call them 'natural' men, or 'unspiritual' men (RSV) – the language he uses in 2:14 – 'The unspiritual man does not receive the gifts of the Spirit of God, for they are folly to him, and he is not able to understand them because they are spiritually discerned.' He does not call them 'natural' or 'unspiritual' because he does not deny that they possess the Spirit. But he cannot call them *spiritual* men because they are not led and controlled by the Spirit. So he uses this third term, *carnal* men: he is speaking about men who are indwelt by the Spirit, but are not controlled by the Spirit, who are living, as the NIV puts it, in a 'worldly' way.

Now it is significant that their carnality is evidenced, not in some moral sphere, but in the simple fact that they were refusing to grow up. For what these men *were* spiritually was going to have the most profound effect upon the whole work of God in Corinth. 'I could not address you as spiritual men, but as men of the flesh ['carnal' in the KJV], as babes in Christ. I fed you with milk, not solid food; for you were not ready for it; and even yet you are not ready, for you are still of the flesh' (*1 Cor.* 3: 1–3, RSV). This is the apostle's basic burden with these people who are to be God's servants in this situation in Corinth.

We tend to forget that the call to ministers of the gospel to grow does not cease when we are ordained; that our own spiritual growth is not an insignificant thing when we have been called into a congregation or work of our own. Indeed, one of the *most vital factors* about our ministry is the whole issue of our own spiritual growth.

It is an appalling possibility for us as ministers to become stagnant in our own spiritual lives. Yet this most fundamental principle operates, and undergirds the whole of Christian service, that what I *am* largely conditions what I *do*.

That is not true in the same way in other spheres of life. It is not true in the 'professions'. For example, here is a man who has become a very distinguished civil engineer, He is now in London and occupies a very senior position with a large international concern; and he has become quite a brilliant engineer. However, the man, who lives in comfortable stockbrokers' suburbia in London, is suddenly exposed in a scandal as having lived a totally double life. His family situation, which seemed to be perfectly happy and normal, was a front for appalling moral disaster; it is a major scandal. But none of this has, apparently, impaired his professional competence, because it seems it is possible to divorce what the man is in secret from what he does in the public sphere. You can never do that in the ministry and in the service of God, because what a man *is* largely determines what he *does*.

E. M. Bounds writes of this at the beginning of his little book *Power through Prayer* – if you do not know it, I would certainly suggest to you that you should read it at least once. He writes:

> We are constantly on a stretch, if not on a strain, to devise new methods, new plans, new organisations, to advance the Church and secure enlargement and efficiency for the Gospel. This trend of the day has a tendency to lose sight of the man, or sink the man in the plan or organisation. God's plan is to make much of the man, far more of him than of anything else, for men are God's methods. The Church is looking for better methods, whereas God is looking for better men. This vital, urgent truth is one that this age of machinery is apt to forget and the forgetting of it is as baneful in the work of God as would be the striking of the sun from his sphere. What the Church needs today is not more machinery, or better; not new organisations or more and novel methods, but men whom the Holy Ghost can use. The Holy Ghost does not flow through methods but through men. He does not come on machinery but on men. He does not anoint plans but men – men of prayer. It is not great talents, nor great learning, nor great preachers that God needs, but men great in holiness; great in faith, great in love, great in fidelity, great for God. These men can mould a whole generation for God.[1]

From an entirely different sphere, Helmut Thielicke makes a similarly shrewd observation in his book *The Trouble with the Church*:

> If I'm not much mistaken, the man of our generation has a very sensitive instinct for routine phrases. Advertising and propaganda have thoroughly accustomed him to this. He knows that the 'ad' man's commendations of a brand-name

---

[1] E. M. Bounds, *Power through Prayer*, London: Marshall (no date), pp. 9–10.

product do not express the personal conviction of the man who is speaking, but that they are the stereo-typed mechanical phrases which are intended to wear a hole in a stubbornly stony 'psyche' by means of a constant drip. Anybody who wants to know whether a particular soft drink is really as good as the advertising man on the T.V. screen says it is, cannot simply believe the phonetically amplified recommendations, but must find out whether this man actually drinks the stuff at home, when he is not in public.

Does the preacher himself drink what he hands out in the pulpit? This is the question that is being asked by the child of our time, who has been burned by publicity and advertising. The fact that he works hard on his preaching, that he studies the Bible and ponders theological problems, this would still be no proof that he drinks his own soft drink. The question is rather whether he quenches his own thirst with the Bible; and if I see a breach, if I see no connection between his Christian and his human existence – so argues the average person consciously or unconsciously – then I am inclined to accept the conclusion that he himself is not living in the house of his own preaching but has settled down somewhere beside it, and that the centre of gravity in his life lies somewhere else.[1]

I find that a very challenging idea: 'the centre of gravity of your life'. Is it in the thing which is the burden of your preaching?

The particular expressions of the carnality of which the apostle speaks here are jealousy and strife. That is very interesting. 'You are still of the flesh. For while there is jealousy and strife among you, are you not of the flesh and behaving like ordinary men?' (*1 Cor.* 3:3, RSV).

[1] H. Thielicke, *The Trouble with the Church*, London: Hodder & Stoughton, 1966, pp. 3, 6.

One of the marks of refusing to grow up is the persistence of jealousy and strife. The centre of a baby's world is self; he expects to be the centre of everybody else's world, and if he is not, at a certain age, if he is very small, he will scream; and if he is a little older, he will throw a tantrum, because he wants to be the centre of the world.

This jealousy, strife and quarrelsomeness, is something, I think, which has a sinister influence when it comes to the service of God, because of the spirit of resentment which goes with it. It is a real test of character (for me anyway, and I imagine for others also), to ask: 'Can I truly and genuinely be really glad when God is blessing and using someone else in a way that he is not blessing and using me, because my consuming passion is for the honour and glory of the name of God, and not just for my own little show?' Jealousy, strife, and this sense of resentment can so often build up, and be destructive in the ministry. It is a danger sign in Christian service when the great green-eyed monster begins to appear in our spirits. It sours and spoils everything, and we need to beware of it as we beware of the devil himself.

Adoniram Judson, the great missionary who went to Burma, wrote this when he left Andover Theological Seminary in the United States, and sailed for Serampore: 'I crave from God such a pure zeal for His glory that I may have a holy disinterest in whom He uses so long as the dear name of my Saviour is honoured here and His kingdom grows.'

That is something which I think is tremendously important.

It was part of the divine wisdom (perhaps even gentle divine humour) when God took Robert Murray M'Cheyne from Dundee and sent him on a trip to the Holy Land, and then brought in young William Chalmers Burns from Kilsyth to Dundee at the very time when he intended to pour out his Spirit in revival on M'Cheyne's congregation. And it was the most beautiful evidence of M'Cheyne's character that he gloried in what God had done.

The same M'Cheyne wrote to Dan Edwards, who was ordained to a ministry amongst the Jews on the 2nd October, 1840:

> I trust you will have a pleasant and profitable time in Germany. I know you will apply hard to German; but do not forget the culture of the inner man – I mean of the heart. How diligently the cavalry officer keeps his sabre clean and sharp; every stain he rubs off with the greatest care. Remember you are God's sword, His instrument, I trust a chosen vessel unto Him to bear His name. In great measure, according to the purity and perfections of the instrument, will be the success. It is not great talents God blesses so much as great likeness to Jesus. A holy minister is an awful weapon in the hand of God.[1]

Now we dare not live under the delusion that anything other than that lies at the very roots of true prosperity in the ministry. That does not, of course, mean that God rewards us because we are good, and withdraws himself from us when we are not. But it does mean that there is a law in the kingdom of God that our character matters to God, and therefore we need to guard our own souls.

To be very practical, guarding your own soul has a lot to do with guarding your mornings. Most of us who have come through school into University and then into the ministry, have this great problem: we have never had anybody to tell us: 'Get down to your desk at 9 a.m.'

Not necessarily at 4 a.m.! Someone once told me that he had suddenly discovered that John Wesley got up at 4 o'clock in the

[1] Andrew A. Bonar (ed.), *Memoir and Remains of Robert Murray M'Cheyne* (first published 1844, reprinted from the 1892 edition, London: Banner of Truth, 1966), p. 282.

morning, and he was vowing a vow to God that *he* was going to get up at that time. I said to him, 'I don't think you have read the other bit. You should really have gone back a page and you would have found that he went to bed at 9 o'clock at night!' But the main point is this: there is an absolutely vital principle in guarding your mornings, because one of the grave dangers of the ministry as I see it (and I see it in myself, in my own life) is the danger of becoming masters in the ignoble art of 'pottering' or trifling.

Charles Simeon who ministered in Holy Trinity Church, Cambridge from 1783 until 1836, and had such an enormous influence among young men in his generation in the Church of England, had a portrait of Henry Martyn in his vestry – it still hangs there. That portrait, Simeon said, always said to him, 'Don't trifle!'

This is something which I think we need to get right in the early years. It is the biggest battle in the world for most ministers. One of the first things to spell out with the utmost clarity to yourself (and if need be, to your congregation too) is what your mornings are *for*. Your mornings are to be spent in your study, by and large, so that there you may come to know God.

Now you will do that in the ordinary business of preparation, of course; it is never divorced from this. One of the glorious privileges of studying the Scriptures in order to bring bread to others, is that there is seed for the sower as well as bread for the eater (*Isa.* 55:10). But the great business of the hours in the study is that you are shut in there as much as is possible, with God.

So, the first principle is: *God's primary concern is with the worker rather than with the work.* And the second is that

THIS WORK IS GOD'S WORK, NOT OURS.

Paul now goes on to show (*I Cor.* 3:5–9), within the great balance of Scripture, that although God makes much of the man in the sense of being concerned with his character, he uses the man who is ready to be nothing, so that the excellency of the power may be of God and not of man.

Thus, having spoken of this jealousy and strife expressing itself in this form in verse 4, 'I belong to Paul', and 'I belong to Apollos', Paul now deals with what is really wrong.

'What is Paul?' he asks. Not, notice, '*Who* is Paul?' The interrogative pronoun is neuter. As J. B. Lightfoot says, 'The neuter gender is exceedingly derogatory.'[1] He asks, 'What thing is Paul?' and 'What thing is Apollos?' And he answers the question, ridiculing this tendency to make much of men, 'They are *diakonoi*, they are servants.' The word is not used here in any technical sense; it is really the word originally for a waiter at the table, and then came to be used of people who were in service generally. Leon Morris says it is a word which stresses the lowly character of the service rendered. Paul uses the term for the simple reason that he is deeply sensitive about anything that would detract or distract from the centrality of the glory of God in the work of God. 'Let him who boasts, boast of the Lord' (*1 Cor.* 1:31, RSV).

What he is really saying, when he asks: 'What is Paul? What is Apollos?' is: They are 'not anything' (verse 7). 'Neither he who plants, nor he who waters is anything.' They are nothing! Only God is anything in this work, and in it God is everything. 'He who plants and he who waters are equal, and each shall receive his wages' (verse 8), 'but neither he who plants, nor he who waters is anything, but only God who gives the growth' (verse 7).

It is God who gave the ministry (verse 5). What then is Paul? What is Apollos? 'Servants through whom you believed, as the Lord assigned to each.' It may be that he is talking about the assigning of a ministry, or about the gift of faith. God gave the ministry. God gave the faith. Both are true. God also gives the

---

[1] Quoted by John Stott in *The Keswick Week 1963*, London: Marshall, Morgan & Scott, 1963, p. 93.

growth. And God also gives the reward to the labourer. So that from beginning to end this work is God's work, not ours. Paul plants, Apollos waters, but the life-giving increase comes from God, and from God alone.

The whole emphasis of this paragraph is on God, and on God at the centre of his work. I think the AV is therefore wrong when it translates verse 9, 'Labourers together with God'. True though that is, Paul's emphasis is not that we are working with God, but that God is working through us and we are fellow-workers. He has chosen us, he has commissioned us, assigned us a task, given us a ministry. He gives men faith. He is the one who resurrects to new life. He is the one who gives growth in the work and we are his fellow-workers. We are fellow-workers; *God's* field; *God's* building. Paul is piling expression upon expression to convince them of this.

One of the things that I find myself having to ask God to remind me about constantly is that, left to ourselves, we *can* do all kinds of things. We can interest people. We can influence them. We can indoctrinate them and educate them. But only God can *regenerate* them. Only God can recreate and renew them so that they are changed from common clay into the very image of Jesus. Only God can do that. Nobody else in the universe can. All your skill, all your gifts, all your academic training, and all your reputation (especially your reputation), will never touch that sphere. It is God's sphere.

There is one thing God will never do. He will never let you interfere with his glory, because he is jealous for it. And if you and I neglect or play down this truth, he will be displeased with us, because the Lord our God is a jealous God. This is where jealousy is meant to reside, in the heart of God, and in our hearts correspondingly, for that same glory. To learn this is probably one of the chief things in the service of God. Recognizing this should produce two results in us, according to Paul: humility before God (verse 7), and equality before one another (verse 8). These are two very important qualities.

Humility before God (verse 7): 'Neither he who plants, nor he who waters is anything, but only God . . .'

Humility is one of the most difficult things to talk about, isn't it? – even to think about for ourselves, because almost as soon as you think about it you have become self-conscious. Yet I am persuaded that true biblical humility is one of the key elements in true usefulness to God. As I read the history of the church, and see men I know, I think we have our finger here on what is one of the key areas. This is not false self-conscious grovelling, for the fruit of true Christ-like lowliness of heart and spirit is something of which you will be quite unconscious. Yet it is utterly vital. It derives from God being at the centre instead of self being at the centre. That is really what biblical humility is, and that is why it is so costly. It is not an affected thing. It is not the same thing as having a diffident, retiring personality by nature. It has nothing to do with personality. It is something which flows from a deep work of grace.

It is said that Alexander Whyte of Edinburgh had preaching for him on one occasion a young man who was getting a bit of a reputation as a preacher. He had come to Free St George's (as it then was), and he went up into the pulpit full of a sense of what they were all expecting from him, the young luminary. Something went badly wrong, and he was shattered! He made a mess of the whole thing. He forgot what he was going to say, his mind went blank, and it was a disaster. He came down the pulpit steps, a broken-hearted man, and cried to Whyte, 'What went wrong, Sir?' Whyte said to him, 'Well, laddie, if you had gone up the way you came down, you would have had more chance of coming down the way you went up.' How truly Calvin wrote, 'The first step towards serving Christ is to lose sight of ourselves.'[1]

[1] *Commentary on 1 Corinthians*, Calvin Translation Society, Baker, p. 39.

Equality before one another (vere 8). Only God is anything. But the corollary of that is not only humility before God, but equality before one another: 'He who plants and he who waters are equal, and each shall receive his wages according to his labour.' Now, obviously, the same sinister spirit which creates a lack of humility, also creates a lack of equality. The same pride which refuses to give God his place, refuses to give my brother his place. The labours of these two men, Paul and Apollos, were different, of course, and one of the troubles with adulating Corinthian congregations was that they were concentrating on the men, Paul and Apollos. But Paul knew that the reward for each lay in God's hands, and therefore the vital thing was that neither of them must affect a superiority over the other.

I think that includes superiority of intellect. None of us imagines that we are all equipped in the same way. What a dull world it would be if it was like that! I think it probably also applies to the superiority of age, although Scripture speaks of a respect which is to be paid to our elders. But I think it is one of the great signs of grace when an older man is able to be yoked in terms of equality with a younger man. It is a sign that something is wrong when this inequality, which basically flows from a lack of humility, makes us unteachable. God sometimes sends the most unusual people to be our teachers – and sometimes the very people that we would resent being taught by. Some of us who are young resent being taught by the old. ('Different generation: doesn't understand the world as it is today!') That is a bad sign. Some of us who are older are unwilling to be taught by those who are younger; but it's so important for us to recognize that the parity of ministers is not just an ecclesiastical principle; it is a biblical requirement, because we are all God's fellow labourers, God's field, God's building. Humility before God will lead to equality before one another, not similarity, or identity with one another. Not that we will ever cease to respect and love, and even admire, the gifts God has given to others, but that we will not affect a superiority, or be oppressed by a sense of inferiority. Our second principle, therefore is: *This work is God's work and not ours.* The third principle is that

GOD'S WORK MUST BE DONE IN GOD'S WAY.

That is, surely, what Paul is beginning to say when he moves the metaphor from the agricultural to the architectural. 'According to the grace of God given to me, like a skilled master builder I laid a foundation' (*1 Cor.* 3:10, RSV).

The master builder – the word is *architecton*, although it is not quite our word 'architect', rather a kind of supervisor of buildings. Notice, Paul attributes his ministry in Corinth again to the grace of God. '*According to the grace of God* given to me, like a wise, skilled master builder I laid a foundation.'

What is particularly impressive here is the ministry that God gave to Paul in Corinth. 'I laid the foundation.' Then somebody else came along and built upon it. This further emphasizes the parity. 'I laid the foundation, and another man is building upon it.' But in the architectural metaphor, the important fact is that Paul gave attention in Corinth to this underlying principle, that the primary test of good building is the patient laying of the right foundation. If we are going to be God's fellow-workers, we will need to do our work God's way. God's way is that buildings are dependent upon the careful laying of true foundations.

At the end of the Sermon on the Mount, Jesus applies this metaphor in terms of character and personal obedience. He paints a graphic picture of two men who were building houses. He is speaking of building obedience into our character – becoming those who hear the Word and *do* it. One puts up his building in no time. Everybody passing by is profoundly impressed at what the man has done. Then here on the other side is this man who is disappearing gradually from public view altogether: he is digging a hole, and he goes down and down and down! People passing by might well say, 'What a great job this fellow's making, and what an edifice, and in no time at all, too. But what this silly fool's doing down his hole, nobody can tell!'

But you see, he was building on a principle that Paul takes up and God underlines as the principle for building in the cause of God and of eternity. The patient laying of the right foundation is what really matters, and you and I, indeed all of us, are going to be tested on this level. You see, it is so easy for us to be drawn away from this principle for all sorts of reasons, and to neglect the foundations and to try to start immediately on the edifice. The terrible thing about that man's edifice, incidentally, was that it was a great outward show with no foundation, and when the testing time came the whole building collapsed.

The foundation of which Paul is speaking is quite specific. We do not need to wonder what he is talking about because, in Acts 18, Luke records exactly what happened when Paul came to Corinth. He had a very rough time there. 'When Silas and Timothy arrived from Macedonia, Paul was occupied with preaching, testifying to the Jews that the Christ was Jesus. And when they opposed and reviled him, he shook out his garments and said to them, "Your blood be upon your own heads: I am innocent. From now on I will go to the Gentiles." And he left there and went to the house of a man named Titius Justus, a worshipper of God; his house was next door to the synagogue' (*Acts* 18: 5–7, RSV). Then Crispus, the ruler of the synagogue, believed on the Lord, and they had to get a new ruler for the synagogue, who turned out to be Sosthenes (verse 17). Then they all came to Paul and began to besiege him, and Paul, obviously a man with a very sensitive spirit – I often think that this mighty giant of a man was extremely sensitive – was frightened! In the middle of the night God came to him in that beautiful moment, with this magnificent testimony to the doctrine of election. He said to him, 'Paul, do not be afraid. I have much people in this city.' Much people in this city! Well, they hadn't heard the gospel yet, many of them. They hadn't been converted yet. But God said, 'I have much people in this city.' 'Preach on. Stay here.' Paul stayed there, and went into the house where he remained a year and six months, teaching the Word of God among them (*Acts* 18:9–11).

Then there was further persecution and God wonderfully overruled it, because he saw a man who was set upon doing God's work God's way: 'After this Paul stayed *many days longer*, and then took leave of the brethren and sailed for Syria' (verse 18).

We need to be clear that we will not be diverted from this kind of ministry: a patient laying of foundations. You may not see anything very much. Don't expect not to see *anything*, of course, but you may not. And other people may not see very much, and you may become sensitive about that. 'What's so-and-so doing in – What's it called? – these days? He doesn't appear to be doing much.' Well, if he is laying foundations, he is doing what really matters.

So go on doing it and, in God's name, do not be diverted from it: the patient teaching of the Word. Remember this fact: our Lord Jesus at the outset of his ministry endured the temptation of the devil to take short cuts to proper ends. 'Throw yourself down from the temple, Come and worship me and all the kingdoms of the world will be yours.' He refused short cuts to proper ends.

To summarize our conclusions so far:

(1) God's primary concern is with the worker rather than with the work.

(2) This work is God's work and not ours.

(3) God's work must be done in God's way.

The fourth principle is:

GOD'S WORK DONE IN GOD'S WAY INVOLVES GREAT COST AND CORRESPONDING REWARD.

We have already hinted at that, as Paul has done. He goes on to talk about different kinds of building (*1 Cor.* 3:12). Notice the principle: 'According to the grace of God given to me, as a skilled master builder I laid a foundation, and another man is building on it. Let each take care how he builds upon it' (verse 10).

> For no other foundation can anyone lay than that which is laid, which is Jesus Christ. Now if anyone builds on the foundation [he describes the materials] with gold, silver, precious stones, or wood, hay, straw [or stubble] – each man's work will become manifest; for the Day will disclose it, because it will be revealed with fire, and the fire will test what sort of work each one has done (*1 Cor.* 3:11–13, RSV).

These two ways of building involve two kinds of materials. They are distinguished in two ways: one is *costly*, the other is *cheap*. Gold, silver and precious stones are costly materials; wood, hay and straw are cheap materials. The other distinction is that one is *permanent*, and the other is *temporary*. Gold, silver and precious stones last. The fire only purifies them. But fire consumes wood, hay and straw; they are temporary.

The simple point is of course that building something of eternal worth is always enormously costly. There is no telling in which way it is going to be costly for each of us, but it is going to be costly to build for eternity. You can build a certain way, of course, that might impress the whole evangelical world and avoid the real cost, but it will be shoddy building. If you are going to build for eternity, it will be costly beyond all telling. And the Judgment Day – what Paul here calls simply 'the Day' – will disclose it.

We may even be able to disguise the kind of building we have been constructing, in some ways – although not from discerning people, I would think – but 'the Day' will declare it. Then everything that is cheap and shoddy will be tried, tested, and burned up.

The cost will be great in terms of all sorts of things. In terms of time, it is important early on in pastoral life that, when you find your time is being 'imposed upon', you and your wife (if you're married) should learn from God how to be delivered from the kind of resentment that simmers when you feel your time is being intruded on. I think that is very important because, you know, there is nothing worse than giving time to people from a heart that resents it and is almost hating them all the time.

One of my favourite missionary ladies is Amy Carmichael, a woman with a beautiful mind, who bore so much suffering in her service in India, where she spent most of her ministry on her back. Writing on these words, 'Always bearing about in the body the dying of the Lord Jesus, that the life also of Jesus may be manifest in our mortal flesh' (*2 Cor.* 4:10), she says:

Jesus, Redeemer and my one Inspirer;
Heat in my coldness, set my life aglow.
Break down my barriers; draw, yea, draw me nigher,
Thee would I know, whom it is life to know.

Deepen me; rid me of the superficial:
From pale delusion set my spirit free.
All my interior being quick unravel;
Pluck forth each thread of insincerity.

Thy vows are on me: Oh, to serve Thee truly,
Love perfectly, in purity obey –
Burn, burn, O Fire; O Wind, now winnow throughly,
O Sword, awake against the flesh and slay.

O that in me,
Thou my Lord
may see of the travail of Thy soul,
And be satisfied. [1]

That is the real cost of effective service. 'Death works in us, but life in you' (*2 Cor.* 4:12).

But there is a reward to it. 'If the work which any man has built on the foundation survives, he will receive a reward. If any man's work is burned up, he will suffer loss, though he himself will be saved, but only as through fire' (*1 Cor.* 3:14–15, RSV). Here there is, of course, the sobering question of what that loss must mean (and that question is scarcely answerable); but what I want to stress for the moment is the *reward:* the reward in glory. For this reward in glory is projected back into time, and begins to be experienced here in this world.

This has been my experience, at least. I have sometimes found myself in my study in the mornings, engaged with the Scriptures, saying to myself, 'What an astonishing thing, to be paid for doing this!' What a mystery it is that you should be paid to do this kind of work!

'Going into the ministry', as Dick Lucas once said to a group of ordinands, 'is like being made Moses' mother; doing what is nearest to your heart and being paid for it.'

There is such reward, and such glory in serving God. We need to communicate this a little bit more to people (if it is real to ourselves), instead of the impression that we so often convey – that it is all agony. For it is not all agony. There is glory in the service of God. There is privilege and wonder in it. We need to catch the sense of that privilege. We need to get hold of this: 'O God, fancy rewarding me for doing this!'

[1] Amy Carmichael, *'God's Missionary'*, London: SPCK, 1957, pp. 25–6.

And the privilege of it grows, as the years go by – as does the sheer wonder that God has permitted us to be his fellow labourers. May he help us increasingly to be that.

15

A PLEA FOR REVIVAL

*T*HE PLACE OF PRAYER in every true revival of religion is as much logical as theological. If revival is a sovereign work of God, as we would declare it to be, then the calling of the people of God in relation to revival is to pray for it. In that sense, prayer is fundamental to revival both biblically and historically.

But it is important at the beginning of our thinking on this theme to see the danger of making a false connection between prayer and revival, in which we could easily fall into the kind of error Charles Grandison Finney exemplified. He said that it was possible for God's people to have a revival at any time or place simply by fulfilling certain conditions. We can find ourselves thinking that prayer is a lever which inevitably produces revival, so that all we need to do if we want to see a revival is arrange a concert of prayer (as they did in the eighteenth century) or all-night prayer meetings (as people have done at other times), and revival will come.

That is a form of the antiquarian fallacy which sees that before any extraordinary work of grace in history, God's people were put to prayer in an extraordinary way. From this we wrongly conclude that if we do as they did, we will experience what they experienced as a matter of course.

Calvin Colton, an American minister of the nineteenth century, wrote quite properly in his book *The History and Character of American Revivals* that a revival:

is a special and manifest outpouring of the Spirit of God, when the work no longer labours in the hands of man but seems to be taken up of God himself . . . the people are then seen rushing in unwonted crowds and under the deepest solemnity to the house of prayer . . .[1]

The proper connection between prayer and revival is also expressed by Jonathan Edwards in his book, *Some Thoughts concerning the Present Revival of Religion in New England* (1742):

So is God's will, through his wonderful grace, that the prayers of his saints should be one great and principal means of carrying on the designs of Christ's kingdom in the world. When God has something very great to accomplish for his church, it is his will that there should precede it the extraordinary prayers of his people; as is manifest by Ezekiel 36:37: 'I will yet, for this, be inquired of by the house of Israel, to do it for them.' And it is revealed that, when God is about to accomplish great things for his church, he will begin by remarkably pouring out the spirit of grace and supplications, Zech. 12:10.[2]

Special prayer for revival is therefore a spirit that God pours out upon his people. It results from a new zeal for God's honour and glory manifested in his church and a recognition that he alone is able to deal with the moribund condition in which the church is often found.

---

[1] C. Colton, *The History and Character of American Revivals*, London: Westley & David, 1832, p. 80.

[2] Jonathan Edwards, *Some Thoughts concerning the Present Revival of Religion in New England*, in *The Works of Jonathan Edwards* (1834, repr. Edinburgh: Banner of Truth, 1974), vol. 1, p. 426. Also reprinted as *Thoughts on the New England Revival*, Edinburgh: Banner of Truth, 2005. See p. 278.

THE WORK OF PRAYER

When God is about to do a remarkable work the universal pattern is, as Robert Murray M'Cheyne is reported to have said, that he persuades people to take up 'the work of prayer'. Although we recognize God's sovereignty in revival, as in all else, we also recognize that a true understanding of God's sovereignty does not encourage human lethargy. The proper response of the people of God to the doctrine of the sovereignty of God is not to shrug their shoulders, but to supplicate the throne of God fervently.

Professor O. Hallesby, in his little book *Prayer*, has these striking words:

> We long for revivals; we speak of revivals; we work for revivals, and we even pray a little for them. But we do not enter upon that labour in prayer which is the essential preparation for every revival . . .
>
> The work of the Spirit can be compared to mining. The Spirit's work is to blast to pieces the sinner's hardness of heart and his frivolous opposition to God. The period of the awakening can be likened to the time when the blasts are fired. The time between the awakenings corresponds, on the other hand, to the time when the deep holes are being bored with great effort into the hard rock. To bore these holes is hard and difficult work, a task which tries one's patience. To light the fuse and fire the shot is not only easy but very interesting work. One sees 'results' from such work. It creates interest, too: shots resound and pieces fly in every direction!

But, Hallesby then adds, tellingly, 'It takes trained workmen to do the boring. Anybody can light a fuse.'[1]

---

[1] Ole Hallesby, *Prayer*, trans. C. J. Carlsen, Inter-Varsity Press, 1948, pp. 63–4.

We need to learn a great deal more about the work that is involved in prayer. Prayer is the essence of the work to which God calls us. We frequently speak about praying *for* the work, but essentially it is prayer which is the real work. There is no harder or more demanding ministry.

The best way to approach this theme is to consider a biblical example of a man pleading with God for the reviving of his cause. It is in the Psalms that we find these pleas most frequently. Sometimes they are very brief: 'Rise up and help us' (*Psa.* 44:26); 'Will you not revive us again, that your people may rejoice in you?' (*Psa.* 85:6); 'Oh, that salvation for Israel would come out of Zion!' (*Psa.* 14:7). Throughout the whole of the Psalter we find God putting such longings into the hearts of his people. Here and there we find special pleas for revival. Psalm 44 is one such. In this Psalm arguments are heaped up and reach a crescendo in the burning appeal of verse 23: 'Awake, O Lord! Why do you sleep? Rouse yourself! Do not reject us forever.'

Nowhere do we find a more extensive or elaborately argued plea for revival than in the eighty-ninth Psalm. Studied with a little care, it is particularly instructive.

The theme of this Psalm is the sharp and painful contrast which the psalmist sees between the covenanted mercies of God and his people's present moribund and desolate condition. He cries out, 'You have renounced the covenant with your servant and have defiled his crown in the dust. You have broken through all his walls and reduced his strongholds to ruins' (verses 39–40).

The psalmist saw the presence of God withdrawn: 'How long, O Lord? Will you hide yourself forever?' (verse 46). He saw the anger and displeasure of God turned toward his people: 'How long will your wrath burn like fire?' (verse 46). Above all, he was incited to cry because he saw the honour of God being reproached in the world. He felt keenly '. . . the taunts with which your enemies have mocked, O LORD, with which they have mocked every step of your anointed one' (verse 51).

The Psalm divides into four sections. Verses 1–18 are concerned with the praise of God for his covenanted mercies. Verses 19–37 are a rehearsal of the terms of God's covenant. In verses 38–45 there is a dark and painful contrast with the present situation. Finally, verses 46–52 are an urgent plea to God to manifest himself and vindicate his honour.

PLEADING GOD'S CHARACTER

The Psalm opens with a burst of praise: 'I will sing of the Lord's great love for ever; with my mouth I will make your faithfulness known through all generations.' When you consider the condition of God's people, described from verse 38 onwards, this is quite remarkable. The psalmist is speaking out of a situation in which he sees the people and cause of God languishing. Yet he begins by magnifying the name and honour of God and expressing his wonder at God's great faithfulness and steadfast love. This teaches us that even when we are in days of great darkness, deeply burdened for the cause of God, all our thinking and all our crying to God must be from a posture of worship. That is one of the great characteristics of the Psalms written in such periods.

The classic example is Job. In the days of his great humiliation he rent his garments, shaved his head as a sign of his distress, and then – notice this carefully – fell upon his face and *worshipped God*, crying, 'The LORD gave and the LORD has taken away; may the name of the LORD be praised' (*Job* 1:21).

The psalmist is convinced that God is always worthy of praise, not just at the time when he is pleasing us. He has not changed! It is we who have changed. He abides faithful. The psalmist says his love is 'great' and 'stands firm for ever'. Notice how frequently the words 'all generations' and 'for ever' appear in these verses. They mean that the writer is praising the unchangeable character of God. Nor is that only the *posture* from which he prays; it is also the very *stimulus* he has to call upon God in this bleak period. He recognizes that God is unchanging in his infinite majesty and in the glory of his character.

It is important to notice the kind of man who effectively pleads with God to revive his cause. He is a man whose soul is stirred and enlarged by the limitless glories of God. This is what he focuses on from verse 5 onwards. 'The heavens praise your wonders, O LORD, your faithfulness too, in the assembly of the holy ones. For who in the skies above can compare with the LORD? Who is like the LORD among the heavenly beings? . . . O LORD God Almighty, who is like you?' (verses 5, 6, 8). 'You rule over the surging sea' (verse 9). 'You crushed Rahab like one of the slain' (verse 10). 'The heavens are yours, and yours also the earth; you founded the world and all that is in it' (verse 11).

This is a pattern of how God teaches his people to plead with him. If you make a study of the prayers of the Bible, you will discover that when God's people recognize themselves to be in great need they become preoccupied with the greatness of God in creation, history, and nature. This enlarges their hearts to call upon him.

Again, this is used by God as an argument to persuade his people to trust him. You find it in Isaiah: 'Why do you say, O Jacob, and complain, O Israel, "My way is hidden from the LORD; my cause is disregarded by my God?" Do you not know? Have you not heard? The LORD is the everlasting God, the Creator of the ends of the earth. He will not grow tired or weary, and his understanding no one can fathom. He gives strength to the weary and increases the power of the weak' (Isa. 40:27–29).

Have you ever noticed how frequently God says, 'I am the God of Abraham, the God of Isaac, and the God of Jacob', or, 'I am the

God who brought your fathers up out of the Red Sea.' Why does God speak this way? The people knew that he had done it, but he is persuading them from his past dealings with them to trust him and come to him again. This rich view of God is the ground on which we plead with him to revive his cause.

PRAYER PROVOKED BY PROMISES

In verses 19–37 the psalmist moves on from pleading God's character to pleading God's covenanted promises. This passage has a close relation to 2 Samuel 7:8–16. It teaches us two general lessons about prayer for revival.

First, prayer for the restoration of God's people is prayer which is *led by Holy Scripture*, for the psalmist reviews what God has said (verse 19). This is both the stimulus and boundary of prayer. As we call upon God, he illumines our understanding by Holy Scripture, and thus teaches us to pray. Where do we discover the glories of God's character which we plead before him? It is in Holy Scripture. For this reason, when God creates prayer warriors he begins by making them Bible students.

The *second* lesson from these verses about prayer for revival is that *God delights to be reminded of his promises:* 'You said, "I have made a covenant with my chosen one"' (verse 3); 'Once you spoke in a vision' (verse 19). Notice the many times he says 'I will' from verse 23 onwards: 'I will crush his foes before him . . . I will set his hand over the sea . . . I will also appoint him my firstborn . . . I will maintain my love to him forever . . . I will establish his line forever . . . if his sons forsake my law and do not follow my statutes . . . I will punish their sin with the rod . . . but I will not take my love from him . . . I will not violate my covenant . . . I will not lie to David.' Robert Murray M'Cheyne used to say, 'Every "I will" on God's lips should become a "Wilt thou . . . ?" on our lips, for promises should provoke prayers.'

In these verses the psalmist is speaking of the election and anointing of David: 'I have found David my servant; with my sacred oil I have anointed him' (verse 20). But it is also a clear picture of the election and anointing of 'great David's greater Son', the Lord Jesus Christ. When the Father covenants with him he covenants with his elect in him. Thus, 'I will maintain my love to him forever, and my covenant with him will never fail. I will establish his line forever, his throne as long as the heavens endure' (verses 28, 29). The covenant means that God's anointed will triumph. Verses 30–34 tell us that although the elect will be chastened when they sin, they will not utterly fall away: 'I will not violate my covenant or alter what my lips have uttered' (verse 34). God is saying that his Word is absolutely reliable, that he never goes back upon it. His Word will last forever.

Jonathan Edwards said, 'For, undoubtedly, that which God abundantly makes the subject of his *promises*, God's people should abundantly make the subject of their *prayers*.'[1]

JEALOUSY FOR THE NAME OF GOD

Verses 38–45 are the third great movement of the Psalm. Using the truth he has already cited, the psalmist now expostulates with God concerning the present condition of his people. Their condition does not bring honour to God's name: 'You have rejected, you have spurned, you have been very angry with your anointed one. You have renounced the covenant with your servant and have defiled his crown in the dust' (verse 38). The psalmist does not pretend that the situation is better than it appears to be.

It is vital that we learn this lesson from the psalm. Since the psalmist does not try to touch up the picture, neither should

---

[1] *The Works of Jonathan Edwards* (1834, repr. Edinburgh: Banner of Truth, 1974), vol. 2, p. 291, in *An Humble Attempt to Promote . . . Extraordinary Prayer for the Revival of Religion and the Advancement of Christ's Kindom on Earth* (1748) .

we. It is not only permissible but our bounden duty to compare what God is doing with what he has promised in his Word. When his providences do not seem to match his promises, our duty is not to remain inactive and unmoved but to emulate the psalmist by fervent intercession that God would make himself known.

Maurice J. Roberts writes on this Psalm:

If God is not manifestly blessing his church but rather giving her over to reproaches and to disgraceful weakness, then it is an expression of our love to him to be fired with holy boldness and to expostulate with him on the basis of his covenant pledges to us as his people. If he has infallibly declared that the gates of hell shall never prevail to destroy the church, must we not expostulate with him when he permits us now great inroads of the powers of darkness upon us? If God has given Christ the heathen for his inheritance, can we remain dumb in our prayer life about the countless multitudes perishing around us? If the Lord has called preaching the wisdom of God and the power of God, can we dispassionately allow sermon after sermon to be preached with no appearance of that wisdom or power in our midst? If God has promised to avenge speedily his elect who cry to him day and night, should we not be exercised with deep concern that mighty answers are not sent to us?[1]

The psalmist grieves because he cares for the honour of the Lord. He knows that the sovereign Lord is jealous for his own glory, and it appears that God is permitting his people to be reproached and shamed. This reflects on him. That is the root of his intercession. The key to his burden is jealousy for the name of God.

---

[1] 'The Prayer for Revival', *Banner of Truth*, No. 61, October 1968, p. 28. Reprinted in *The Thought of God* (Edinburgh: Banner of Truth, 1993), pp. 185–6.

It was this which provoked Paul in his spirit at Athens. He saw the city full of idols and he was 'greatly distressed' (*Acts* 17:16). The various translations of this scarcely do justice to Paul's burden. The word which the NIV renders 'greatly distressed' appears to be sometimes used in Greek medical terminology for a heart attack. Luke is telling us that Paul had a paroxysm of spirit when he saw the glory of the only true God dragged down into the idol worship of Athens.

It is interesting that in the Septuagint[1] this same word is used of God being distressed with Israel for making the golden calf. What provoked God in relation to Israel and Paul in relation to Athens was burning jealousy for God's glory. This is always part of the prelude to revival. History shows that God's people begin to know something of this zeal.

Do you know the story of Henry Martyn, the great young Cambridge scholar, who in his brief life served God in the East translating the Bible into Persian? At one point in his travels he had seen a drawing in which Jesus was represented catching hold of the garments of Mohammed and bowing to him. Martyn was deeply distressed in spirit. He was in tears. When someone asked him what was upsetting him he replied, 'I could not endure existence if Jesus were not to be glorified. It would be hell to me if he were always thus to be dishonoured.'[2]

It is that spirit which I find so lacking in my own soul and in the contemporary evangelical church. We are roused very much these days by pictures of the physical distress of people around the world, and rightly so. But it is a strange thing to me that I can walk through cities like Glasgow or Philadelphia and not find the spirit gripping me which gripped the apostle in Athens, namely zeal for God's honour. We need to ask ourselves why we do not share the

[1] The Greek version of the Old Testament current in the first century.
[2] Constance Padwick, *Henry Martyn, Confessor of the Faith*, (IVF, 1953), p.146.

psalmist's distress over our situation. Is it perhaps because we do not share his zeal for the honour of the name of God which is brought into reproach? Or, if we are distressed over the present situation, do we need to ask whether it is motivated by a care for the honour of God and zeal for his name, or for our reputation and our name?

HOW LONG? HOW LONG?

In the fourth section (verses 46–52) the psalmist pleads that God would turn the tide of events in his own lifetime: 'How long, O LORD? Will you hide yourself forever? How long will your wrath burn like fire?' What the psalmist grieves over and cries to God to turn is his displeasure. He knows that there are things in the life of the people that are causing God's displeasure. He knows that God has in some sense withdrawn himself. So he cries out, 'How long? . . . Will you hide yourself forever?'

There are two grounds for the urgency of this concern: first, the length of time God's cause has languished ('How long, O LORD?'), and second, the brevity of his own life ('Remember how fleeting is my life. For what futility you have created all men! What man can live and not see death, or save himself from the power of the grave?' [verses 47–8]).

He makes this urgent plea on the basis of God's covenant: 'O Lord, where is your former great love, which in your faithfulness you swore to David?' (verse 49). He is reminding God that he has placed himself under obligation to his people. Here is great boldness. But this is an important thing to learn from the psalmist's prayer. There is a distinction to be drawn between God's works for his people being gracious and their being voluntary. All God's works are gracious, but his blessing upon his church is not voluntary, in the sense that God has laid himself under obligation. Someone has said, 'If God has sworn to do us good, then he is bound by the terms of his own infallible veracity and faithfulness to make good his covenanted promise.' That is why we may, so to speak, give him no rest.

In verses 50 and 51 the writer pleads God's honour again. God's honour is bound up with the good of his church; so that the taunts of the psalmist's enemies are actually the taunts of God's enemies. The object of their mockery is God's 'anointed one'. At this point the Psalm comes to an abrupt close. These matters are left with God in the confidence that he will act in due time.

However, there is more than a hint in the Psalm of how God will honour his covenant and vindicate his cause. In verses 50 and 51, as we have just seen, a figure appears under the highly significant names of 'your servant' and 'your anointed one'. It is therefore not surprising that many have seen this Psalm as messianic. Artur Weiser concludes:

> It is true that the promise of God has not become ineffective. It has been fulfilled, not in the person of the king of Israel, but in Christ. And this has been done in a manner which, contrary to all human expectations and beyond all human comprehension, has revealed the miracle of God's ways and judgments which lead to salvation, a miracle so mysterious that even . . . the Apostle Paul, pondering over these problems, can do nothing else but, deeply stirred, confine himself to the adoration of the unsearchable majesty of God (*Rom.* 11:33). The early Christians therefore interpreted the psalm in a Messianic sense, as pointing to Christ.[1]

As Derek Kidner puts it, 'The unanswerable questions . . . were to have . . . unquestionable answers.'[2]

---

[1] Weiser, *The Psalms*, pp. 593–4.
[2] Derek Kidner, *Psalms 73–150* (Tyndale Old Testament Commentary), London: IVP, 1975.

Nothing could be more appropriate at the close of this Psalm than the doxology which in verse 52 concludes Book III of the Psalter:

> Praise to the LORD for ever!
>
> Amen and Amen.

16

LESSONS FOR THE CHURCH ON EARTH FROM THE CHURCH IN HEAVEN

CHAPTERS 21 AND 22 OF REVELATION describe for us the final glory of the church of Jesus Christ. John uses three symbols to express what the glorified people of God are like:

A beautiful bride (Chapter 21:1–8);
A walled city (Chapter 21:9–27); and
A watered garden (Chapter 22:1–5).

These are not so much pictures we are to visualize as symbols we are to interpret. When we do, we find a description of the perfected church in heaven. From that description, we ought to be able to learn some vital lessons about how God is shaping and moulding his people here on earth to conform them to the perfect pattern of the church in glory. Seven of these characteristics stand out:

1. THE PRESENCE OF GOD IS THE CHIEF DELIGHT OF HIS PEOPLE.

In Revelation 21:3, the voice from the throne announces what is really being celebrated in this marriage of the bride. It is that 'The dwelling of God is with men, and he will live with them.

They will be his people, and God himself will be with them and be their God.' The language is reminiscent of the description of the Old Testament tabernacle, the point of which was that God's presence was known among his people. But in heaven there is a multiplied reality about the presence of God, which makes his church delight in him as a bride in her bridegroom. The lesson for God's people in this world is that they need to learn to make God's presence their chief delight here below.

2. THE HOLINESS OF GOD IS THE TRUE BEAUTY OF HIS PEOPLE.

In Revelation 21:2 John sees 'the holy city'. The phrase is repeated in verse 10. Now it is of course of the church that John is speaking. Paul tells us in Ephesians 5:25–27 that 'Christ loved the church and gave himself up for her to make her holy . . . and to present her to himself as a radiant church . . . holy and blameless.' Holiness is one of God's communicable attributes – that is, it is one of the attributes he shares with us. The beautiful dress of the bride as she is adorned for her husband (*Rev.* 21:2) is the beauty of holiness. By contrast, in Revelation 17:4, one of the characteristics of the woman dressed in purple and scarlet, Babylon (representing the godless world), was that she was concerned with glamour rather than with true beauty. The true beauty of the people of God is the holiness with which he adorns them.

3. THE GLORY OF GOD IS THE TRUE GLORY OF HIS PEOPLE.

This perfect holy city of New Jerusalem is a brilliant, shining, sparkling jewel which has a remarkable glory (*Rev.* 21:11, 23). Even the kings of the earth bring their splendour into it, in the sense that they lay it down in tribute before God's glory.

Now if that is the pattern in heaven, the purpose of God in the church here on earth is that everything within it may conspire to reveal his glory. That is to be the unifying ambition behind everything we do.

4. THE TRUTH OF GOD IS THE ONLY FOUNDATION FOR HIS PEOPLE.

'The wall of the city had twelve foundations, and on them were the names of the twelve apostles of the lamb' (*Rev.* 21:14).

The consistent testimony of Scripture is that the foundation of the church of Jesus Christ is apostolic truth. Paul assures the Ephesian Christians that they are 'members of God's household, built on the foundation of the apostles and prophets' (*Eph.* 2:19–20). The walls of the city described in Revelation 21 are obviously of great significance. They are vast in size, some two hundred feet thick. The point is that they give stability and security to the city.

But in Revelation 21:19 we are told that the foundations were recognized as particularly precious by being studded with precious stones of every kind. The lesson is obvious. It is that the stability and security of the church of God depends upon the stability and security of the walls, which in turn depends upon the foundation being truly laid. The supremely precious truth of God given to the apostles by Jesus, and inscripturated in the New Testament, is what constitutes that foundation. Tamper with it or erode it, and you strike a blow at the church's stability.

5. THE THRONE OF GOD IS AT THE CENTRE OF LIFE FOR HIS PEOPLE.

Throughout the book of Revelation the central feature of John's vision of heaven is a throne. In these two chapters, the throne of

God is the centre of gravity of his people's life. That means that obedience to God is their lifestyle. They are described as 'his servants' in Revelation 22:3. That is a pattern which is of the essence of the life of God's people on earth as well as in heaven. It may well be that it is this that Jesus had in mind when he taught us to pray, 'May your will be done on earth as it is in heaven.'

6. THE SUFFICIENCY OF GOD IS THE TRUE NOURISHMENT OF HIS PEOPLE.

At the beginning of Chapter 22, the angel shows John a vision of a river with the water of life flowing clear as crystal down the middle of the great street of the city (*Rev.* 22:1–2). On either side is the tree of life bearing twelve crops of fruit, yielding its fruit every month, and the leaves of the tree are themselves health-giving. It is a picture of the super-abundance of God's supply.

Fancy a tree which provides twelve crops of fruit in the one year! It is the same God who supplies all our needs according to his riches in glory in Christ Jesus (*Phil.* 4:19).

7. THE WORSHIP OF GOD IS THE CONSTANT ACTIVITY OF HIS PEOPLE.

The New International Version translates Revelation 22:3 as 'his servants will serve him', but the RSV is probably nearer to the meaning when it translates, 'his servants will worship him'. Of course, that is what we learn throughout the whole of Revelation. The language of those who surround the throne of God is, 'Worthy is the lamb who was slain, to receive power and wealth and wisdom and strength and honour and glory and praise!' (*Rev.* 5:12). Day and night they never stop saying, 'Holy, holy, holy is the Lord God Almighty, who was, and is, and is to come' (*Rev.* 4:8).

Lessons from the Church in Heaven

As it is the constant activity of the church in heaven, so it is the chief business of the church on earth to bring worship and honour and glory and praise to the name of our great God and Saviour.

If we dream of a revived, renewed church, these are the elements which will appear in it.

Holiness. No one is in your league.

Gods glory Revealed: God is ...
- Call to Worship

~~Mary~~
- Prayer of INVOCATION   IS. 6

Response to Gods glory: We Respond thru

Hymn - keeping with Topic

~~Confession~~
CONFESSION over our SIN →
   - Omission
   - Commission

ASSURANCE of PARDON

Hymn of Praise

~~Gospel~~ Hearing Gods Word God speaks

OT / NT Reading   We Resp
                                          ode
         CONFESS ~~or~~ our faith

MESSAGE — God Speaks

Hymn we Respond
      Benediction — God Speaks

ALSO AVAILABLE FROM THE
BANNER OF TRUTH TRUST

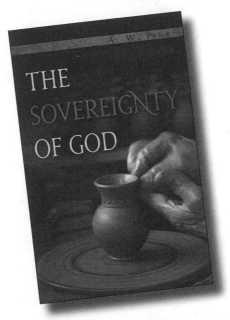

The Sovereignty of God
Arthur W. Pink

'Present day conditions', writes the author, 'call loudly for a new examination and new presentation of God's omnipotence, God's sufficiency, God's sovereignty. From every pulpit in the land it needs to be thundered forth that God still lives, that God still observes, that God still reigns. Faith is now in the crucible; it is being tested by fire, and there is no fixed and sufficient resting-place for the heart and mind but in the throne of God. What is needed now, as never before, is a full, positive, constructive setting forth of the Godhood of God.'

Such a book as this must cause serious thought, but it is not intended to provoke mere intellectual discussion. It should drive us to prayer. It should fill us with joy . . . It should bring more calmness and peace into our daily Christian walk. It should take our eyes off men and fix them on Jesus the name high over all, in earth and sea and sky'.

From the Publishers' Preface

ISBN: 978-1-84871-049-8   168pp.   Paperback

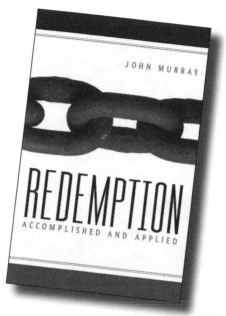

Redemption: Accomplished and Applied
John Murray

The value of John Murray's writing as a theologian has been increasingly recognised in recent years. Here we find the same strong theology, but distilled and expressed for Christians in general rather than for theological students in particular.

Murray deals with the nature and meaning of the death of Christ, and with the way in which the Christian inherits the blessings which flow from it, through regeneration, justification, adoption, sanctification and glorification. There is, he says, 'an unbreakable chain of events proceeding from God's eternal purpose in foreknowledge and predestination to the glorification of the people of God.'

> 'Murray's distinctive . . . is his careful exegesis of Scripture passages, so that his theological assertions come straight from the Word of God with all the authority which that gives them. His treatment of the order of the application of redemption is masterly . . . one of the greatest theological books written in the last hundred years.' [FREE CHURCH WITNESS]

ISBN: 978-1-84871-046-7   200pp.   Paperback

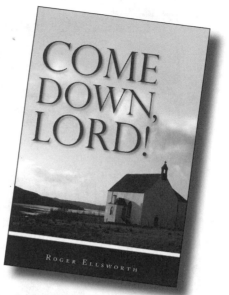

Come Down, Lord!
Roger Ellsworth

Here is a succinct, readable and biblically-based treatment of the vital theme of revival. Taking as his starting place the widespread absence of the sense of God's holy presence and our need of his grace, Roger Ellsworth traces the profound analysis of the church's spiritual decay outlined in Isaiah 63:3–64:12, and applies its message to our times. While calculated to expose our spiritual need, *Come Down, Lord!* will also stimulate repentance, prayer and fresh faith in the promised mercy of God.

This revised edition contains Questions for Discussion at the end of each chapter.

ISBN: 978-1-84871-039-9   64pp.   Paperback

THE BANNER OF TRUTH TRUST

3 Murrayfield Road,
Edinburgh EH12 6EL
UK

P O Box 621, Carlisle,
Philadelphia 17013,
USA

www.banneroftruth.co.uk